Cute Quilts fo

Kristin Roylance

Martingale®
Create with Confidence

Dedication

In honor of my own six cute kids—Jeffrey, Ally, Justin, Savannah, Brooklyn, and Claire. Though some of them are almost grown, they will always be my babies.

And to my supportive husband and biggest fan, Sean. Without his help and willingness to let me follow my dreams, this book would be only that—a dream—and a very large pile of fabric!

Cute Quilts for Kids
© 2014 by Kristin Roylance

Martingale®
19021 120th Ave. NE, Ste. 102
Bothell, WA 98011-9511 USA
ShopMartingale.com

Printed in China
19 18 17 16 15 14   8 7 6 5 4 3 2 1

**Library of Congress Cataloging-in-Publication Data
is available upon request.**

ISBN: 978-1-60468-256-4

Mission Statement

Dedicated to providing quality products and service to inspire creativity.

Credits

PRESIDENT AND CEO: Tom Wierzbicki
EDITOR IN CHIEF: Mary V. Green
DESIGN DIRECTOR: Paula Schlosser
MANAGING EDITOR: Karen Costello Soltys
ACQUISITIONS EDITOR: Karen M. Burns
TECHNICAL EDITOR: Laurie Baker
COPY EDITOR: Sheila Chapman Ryan
PRODUCTION MANAGER: Regina Girard
COVER AND INTERIOR DESIGNER: Regina Girard
PHOTOGRAPHER: Brent Kane
ILLUSTRATOR: Lisa Lauch

Contents

Introduction

I've been blessed to be surrounded by amazing quilters and talented seamstresses all of my life. Some of my earliest memories include a much-loved, ragged, handmade quilt sewn together from soft polyester fabric. That particular blanket accompanied me everywhere I wandered as a young child. I still have it stored safely in my cedar chest. I loved that quilt not only because my grandmother made it, but also because it loved me right back!

While the purpose of baby quilts has remained the same over the years, the style of baby quilts has changed dramatically. Most baby quilts are now made featuring bright, trendy cotton fabric rather than pastel polyester, and most are machine quilted rather than hand quilted. No matter the style, each is made to be loved and used. The patterns in *Cute Quilts for Kids* will stand the test of time, and likely will be gently placed in cedar chests for safekeeping until later generations are able to enjoy them.

Cute Quilts for Kids, just as the name suggests, includes patterns for cute quilts that can be lovingly made for babies and kids! The patterns in this collection all contain ideas for using embellishments that add dimension to the quilts without adding a lot of difficulty for the busy quiltmaker. The quilts are all

easy enough for a beginner, but are fresh enough to entice the veteran quilter. The patterns found in this book are a bit unconventional, and that's what makes them so fun. I'm excited to be able to share my patterns with people that share my two loves: quilting and babies.

Quiltmaking Basics

There are probably as many quilting rules as there are quilters. As your skills increase and your style of quilting evolves, your quilting techniques will most likely change as well. Some basic quiltmaking techniques, however, will be used in every quilt you make.

Fabric Selection

One of the most fulfilling aspects of making a quilt is selecting the fabric. It can also be one of the most intimidating. Here are some helpful hints to remember as you choose fabrics for your quilt.

- Start by picking something that *you* love. It's much easier to start and finish a quilt using materials that inspire you.

- Just like adults, babies and children love bright colors, unique textures, and vibrant contrast. Select one fabric that you love as the main print, and then choose complementary or coordinating fabrics.

- Select a high-quality, 100% cotton fabric. The tighter the weave, the better. Quilts made for babies and small children are likely to be washed—a lot! The fabric needs to hold up to constant washings.

- Plush, polyester microfiber fabrics such as Minky work beautifully for the backing material. While not fun to piece with, a single piece for the backing will make the quilt irresistibly soft.

Fabric Preparation

One of the most common questions I'm asked by fellow quilters is whether or not to wash and dry the fabric before cutting. Quilters all have their own opinion on the subject and no one is more right than anyone else. It's all in the look you prefer. I love the faded, comfortably worn look of antique quilts, so I prefer to create my quilts before washing the fabric. Once washed, the cotton fabric will shrink ever so slightly and give the quilt a bit of soft texture.

Quilting Tools and Supplies

My children have actually referred to me as "Inspector Gadget" because of the arsenal of quilting tools I have at my disposal. You can never have too many tools to make the job quicker, more accurate, and just plain fun. If you only want the essentials, make sure you have the following.

Rotary-cutting supplies. A large cutting mat, a rotary cutter with a sharp cutting blade, and a see-through ruler are critical for accurate cutting. I like to cut from the left edge of the fabric, with the selvage edges matched at the top of the cutting mat. Use the lines on the mat as a guide to keep the fabric and selvage edges straight; cut from the right edge of the ruler.

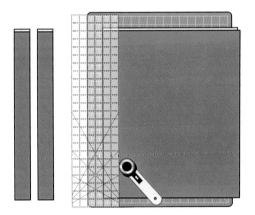

Sewing machine. The sewing machine you use doesn't need to be fancy or have every bell and whistle available (please don't tell my husband), but it does need to sew an accurate straight stitch. Keep your machine in good working order with regular cleanings and maintenance to prolong its life so it'll give you years of sewing pleasure. Be sure to change your needle at the start of every project as well.

Rotary-Cutter Rules

A rotary cutter is an amazing tool for quiltmaking, and it greatly increases the speed and accuracy of cutting. But, the blade is very sharp and needs to be treated with respect. Here are a few critical things to keep in mind when using a rotary cutter.

- Always keep the blade in the locked position between cuts.
- Always cut away from you.
- Walk your hand up the ruler as you cut, being mindful to keep your fingers away from the edge of the ruler.
- Carefully discard used blades to prevent accidental cuts.
- Change your blade often; a sharp blade is more effective than a blade with nicks.

¼" presser foot. An accurate ¼" seam allowance is critical for piecing each quilt. Most machines have a special foot available for this purpose. This special foot is also referred to as a piecing or patchwork foot.

Walking foot. While a walking or even-feed foot isn't required, it can make sewing through multiple layers much easier. I always use the walking foot when applying ruffles and rickrack to my quilts. I also love to use a walking foot when applying binding to the front of the finished quilt. You'll find the fabric layers move easily under the presser foot, and puckers will be a thing of the past. A walking foot will save you frustration and time when sewing many of the quilts in this book.

Walking foot

Ironing board and iron. Pressing is a simple yet important step in quilting. Be sure to have a sturdy ironing board with a clean, functioning iron. Keep your pressing tools in a convenient location or you may be tempted to skip this critical step. I like to have a separate iron that I use only for fusible appliqué. This iron should be cleaned regularly to prevent buildup on its surface, which can easily transfer to your fabrics.

Fusible web. Many of the projects in this book call for fusible web. When choosing fusible web, be sure to select a *lightweight* variety with a paper backing. Sewing through heavy varieties is very difficult and can gum up the needle and cause skipped stitches.

Gridded fusible interfacing. A gridded, nonwoven fusible interfacing, such as Pellon Quilter's Grid, is a great quilting tool. I almost feel like I'm cheating when I use it. (Of course, there's no such thing as cheating in quilting, as long as you get the job done!) The fusible grid comes in 1" increments (both traditional and on point) and makes piecing small squares a snap. Follow the instructions that come with the product and the squares magically fall into place without having to match seams. You may never piece small squares together without it again! I've used this product to make "Are We There Yet?" (page 27); you can also use it to make "Rodeo Roundup" (page 40), "Anchors Aweigh!" (page 16) and "Tromp, Chomp, Stomp!" (page 53).

Water-soluble pen. A good water-soluble pen is a great tool for any quilter. I use it to help with placement of appliqué pieces and dimensional trims. With just a squirt from the water bottle, the lines disappear. I wish fingerprints on windows came off as easily!

Seam ripper. Everyone hates to unpick, and I'm no exception. But a good seam ripper will make that job less frustrating. I have one rule about unpicking—I only unpick a seam once. After that, I deal with how it looks. Too much unpicking will create a weakness in the fabric, and who wants that?

Washable-glue sticks: A washable-glue stick (I use Elmer's) is the perfect tool to use instead of pins for holding small objects onto fabric so you can appliqué or sew them in place. When heat set with a hot iron, the glue dries clear and washes out completely.

Basic Piecing Techniques

Your sewing machine should be set to stitch approximately 11 stitches per inch (about a 2.5 setting on many machines). Remember to start with a new, sharp needle for each project.

I like to use a neutral-colored thread that will work with all the fabrics I'm using when piecing a quilt. It saves an enormous amount of time if you don't have to continually change the thread, giving you more time to sew.

When piecing, place the fabric right sides together and match the edges. I like to pin my pieces together, and then remove the pins right before the sewing-machine needle reaches them. Sewing over pins can cause the sewing-machine needle to break and make the stitch length longer than you desire, plus it can alter your machine's timing.

An accurate ¼"-wide seam allowance will prevent a lot of frustration. Being off by even one thread width can completely change the dimension of a finished quilt, especially if there are several small pieces to be sewn. Use a ¼" presser foot or follow a line on your machine's throat plate that's a scant ¼" from the needle, and perform the following simple test each time you begin sewing. Cut three strips of scrap fabric, 1½" x 3". Sew the strips together along the long edges. Press the seam allowances to one side. The center strip should now measure exactly 1" across. If it doesn't, adjust the needle position or guideline position and test again.

1¼" 1" 1¼"

When sewing across intersecting seam allowances, be sure the seams match up exactly. Some of the intersecting seams will be sewn over open seam allowances, while others will be sewn by butting the edges of the seams against each other. To keep the seam allowances in place while sewing, pin near the intersecting seam and remove the pin right before reaching it.

When piecing, it isn't necessary to backstitch at the beginning and end of the seam, unless stated otherwise. Take advantage of this and piece by continually feeding the next piece to be sewn under the presser foot without cutting the threads and starting again. Chain stitching makes the sewing machine much less likely to jam when starting a new seam and will also save a large amount of thread and time.

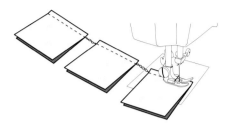

Pressing

Mention ironing to me and I begin to get nervous—my heart races and my palms begin to sweat. My idea of ironing is to throw the garment into a dryer with a damp towel to steam out the wrinkles. You may be surprised to know that despite my dislike for ironing, I own three different irons, and love them all.

Pressing, however, is drastically different from ironing. Pressing is used to heat set a seam, making the seam crisp and clean and giving the pressed seam a flat, straight line. When pressing, it's important to move the iron in an up-and-down motion, not the back-and-forth motion you use for ironing. Finger-press the seam first, and then place the iron directly on the seam. Lift the iron up and off the seam.

An iron is a very valuable tool when appliquéing and adding dimensional trims to many of the quilts featured in this book. One of my very favorite uses for an iron is for heat setting items onto a quilt that have been temporarily adhered with a washable-glue stick. Simply apply the glue to the back of an embellishment, put in place, and secure by pressing down on it with a hot iron. The embellishment can then be easily secured to the quilt by sewing it using a straight stitch or zigzag stitch. Any excess glue can easily be removed with water.

Fusible-Web Appliqué

When I first began my quilting adventures, I looked for patterns that didn't require appliqué. I was very intimidated by the process, and I dragged my feet learning how to do it. Since then, I've discovered appliqué can be quite simple, and I love the designs that can be created. I've tried many different types of appliqué, but my favorite method uses fusible web. There are many different brands of this product. Be sure that the product you purchase has a fusible material on both sides, with one side covered by paper. The quilts in this book use lightweight fusible web so the appliqués can be temporarily adhered with the fusible product, and then permanently stitched in place without gumming up the needle; heavier-weight fusible products are intended to permanently adhere the appliqué without additional stitching, so the fusible product is thicker and can quickly gum up your needle.

When patterns are traced onto fusible web, they need to be the reverse of how they'll appear in the project (if they're not symmetrical). All of the appliqué patterns in *Cute Quilts for Kids* have already been reversed and are ready for tracing.

1. Place the fusible web over the appliqué pattern with the paper side up. Using a pencil, trace the pattern the number of times required, leaving at least ½" between each shape. Roughly cut out the drawn shapes, approximately ¼" from the drawn lines on all sides.

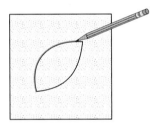

2. Follow the manufacturer's instructions for adhering the fusible-web shape to the wrong side of the fabric you've selected for the appliqué. Don't remove the paper backing yet.

3. Use sharp scissors to cut out the appliqué pieces directly on the drawn lines. Remove the paper backing from each appliqué piece.

4. Follow the project instructions or refer to the order given on the patterns to carefully position the prepared appliqué at the desired location on the background fabric, fusible side down. Press in place following the manufacturer's instructions. Allow the fabric to cool completely.

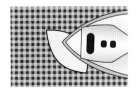

⑤ Use either a zigzag stitch or a satin stitch and matching thread to secure the edges of the appliqué pieces.

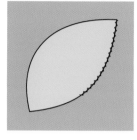 

Zigzag stitch   Satin stitch

Embroidery Stitches

Some of the projects use two common embroidery stitches—a basic backstitch and a running stitch. Use a size 5 embroidery needle and the number of strands of floss indicated in the project instructions to make your stitches.

Backstitch

Pull the needle through from the back to the front at A. Make a small backward stitch entering at B and coming out a bit in front of the first stitch at C. Make the second backward stitch, inserting the needle again at A and coming out a bit in front of the second stitch. Continue in this manner until complete.

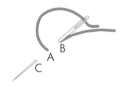

Backstitch

Running Stitch

Bring the needle up from the back at A, down at B, and back up at C. Continue in this manner, pulling the needle in and out of the fabric to make surface stitches that are all the same length. The stitches on the underside should also be equal in length but half the length of the surface stitches.

Running stitch

Finishing Your Quilts

Once the quilt top is complete, you'll need to layer it with batting and backing, and then quilt the layers together and bind the edges.

Prepare the Backing and Batting

Your backing and batting need to be larger than the quilt top to allow for shifting that may occur during the quilting process. Measure your pressed quilt top and add 8" to the length and width measurements to determine the size of your backing and batting.

All of the quilts in this book will require a pieced backing, so you'll need to cut your backing fabric into two lengths and sew the pieces together along the lengthwise grain of the fabric after removing the selvage edges; press the seam allowances open. Trim the backing to the size determined, keeping the seam centered.

Cotton batting works very well for baby quilts. The finished product won't be thick or heavy, and once washed the quilt will have a soft, warm feel that's perfect to cuddle with. You can buy batting by the yard or packaged in specific sizes. Unroll your batting so it lies flat and allow it to rest for at least 24 hours before layering your quilt.

Assemble and Quilt the Layers

The quilts in this book have all been machine quilted on a long-arm quilting machine. I love the finished look of long-arm machine quilting, and the stitches hold up well through frequent washing. Of course, you have the option of hand quilting your quilt or machine quilting it on a home sewing machine as well.

No matter how you choose to quilt your project, begin by looking over the quilt top closely. Trim any threads and press any seams that aren't lying flat. Press the quilt well, being careful not to stretch the edges. If the quilt is being machine quilted by someone else, follow the quilter's instructions. If you or someone else is hand quilting the quilt or you're machine quilting the quilt on your domestic sewing machine, assemble the layers as follows.

① Place the pressed quilt backing wrong side up on a large, flat, clean surface. Smooth it out and secure the edges with masking tape to keep the backing smooth and taut but not stretched.

② Center the batting over the backing and smooth out any creases.

③ Center the pressed quilt top over the batting.

④ Baste the layers together, beginning in the center and working out toward the edges. If you're machine quilting, use rustproof safety pins to hold the layers together. For hand quilting, thread baste the layers together.

⑤ Quilt as desired.

Bind the Edges

Follow the instructions with each project to cut the amount of 2½"-wide binding strips needed.

① Sew the binding strips together end to end to make one long strip. Press the seam allowances open. Press the strip in half lengthwise, wrong sides together and raw edges matching, to create a strip measuring 1¼" wide.

② On one end of the binding strip, press up the corner at the fold of the binding toward the binding raw edges to create a 45° angle. Starting at approximately the middle of one side of the quilt, place the folded end of the binding on the quilt top, aligning the raw edges. Pin the binding in place to the first corner. Make a mark on the binding ¼" from the corner of the quilt top. Using a ¼" seam allowance, sew the binding to the front of the quilt, backstitching at the beginning of the strip and at the ¼" mark. Lift the needle, pull the quilt out from under the presser foot, and clip the threads.

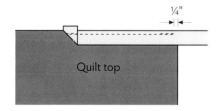

③ Fold the binding strip up toward the edge just sewn, creating a 45° angle. Fold the binding back down, even with the second side of the quilt and keeping the fold intact. Pin the binding in place along this side of the quilt and make a mark ¼" from the next corner. Beginning at the

folded edge, stitch the binding in place, backstitching at the edge and the ¼" mark.

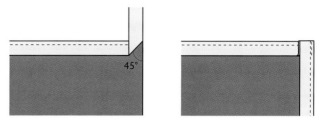

④ Repeat the folding and stitching process at each of the remaining corners. When you're close to the beginning of the binding, overlap the binding ends approximately 2", and then finish stitching the binding in place. Trim away the excess binding strip.

⑤ Trim the batting and backing fabric even with the raw edges of the quilt top. Fold the binding from the front of the quilt over to the back of the quilt along one side and pin in place, making sure to cover the stitching line.

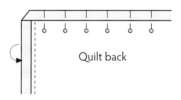

Quilt back

⑥ Working counterclockwise around the quilt, fold over and pin the binding to the remaining sides of the quilt, forming a miter at each corner.

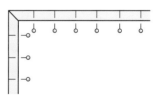

⑦ Blindstitch the binding to the back of the quilt. Be careful that the stitches don't go through to the front of the quilt.

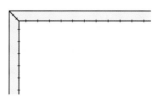

Ladybug Landing

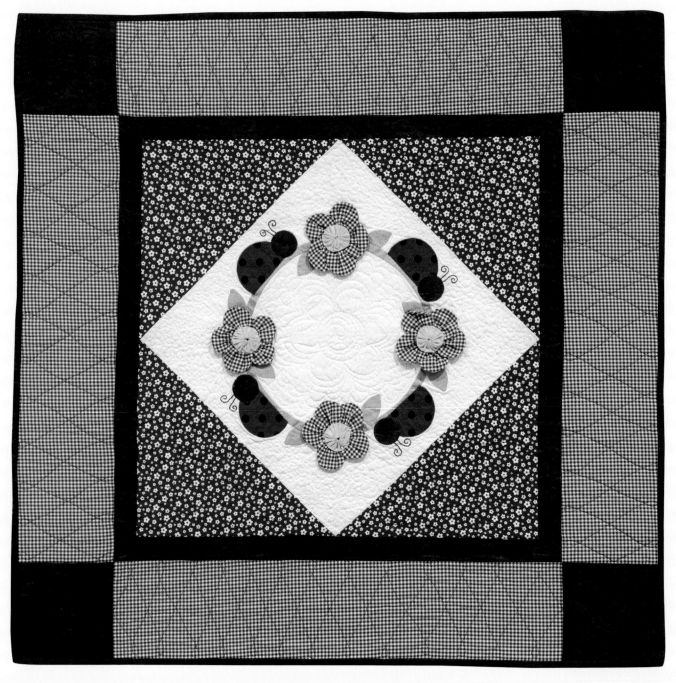

Finished quilt: 40¼" x 40¼"

Pieced by Kristin Roylance; machine quilted by Molly Kohler

Ladybugs and flowers make this quilt almost as much fun as taking a walk in the park!

Materials

Yardage is based on 42"-wide fabric.

⅞ yard of black solid for inner border, outer-border corner squares, ladybug heads, and binding

⅞ yard of red check for outer border and flowers

⅝ yard of white tone on tone for center square

½ yard of red print for setting triangles

12" x 12" square of green solid for stems and leaves

10" x 10" square of yellow tone on tone for flower centers

8" x 8" square of red polka dot for ladybug bodies

2½ yards of fabric for backing

48" x 48" piece of batting

¼ yard of 17"-wide paper-backed fusible web

White, yellow, and black embroidery floss

Size 5 embroidery needle

Template plastic

Water-soluble pen

Cutting

From the white tone on tone, cut:
1 square, 18" x 18"

From the red print, cut:
2 squares, 13¼" x 13¼"; cut in half diagonally to yield 4 triangles

From the black solid, cut:
1 strip, 6½" x 42"; crosscut into 4 squares, 6½" x 6½"
5 strips, 2½" x 42"
2 strips, 2" x 24½"
2 strips, 2" x 27½"

From the red check, cut:
4 strips, 6½" x 27½"

Appliqué the Center Square

1. Refer to "Fusible-Web Appliqué" (page 7) and use the patterns (page 15) to prepare the appliqués from the fabrics indicated.

2. Fold the white 18" square in half diagonally in both directions; press the creases to create alignment lines for the appliqués.

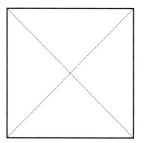

3. Appliqué the stems between the creases on the white square as shown. The ends should come together at the creased lines but not overlap.

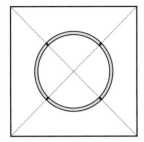

4. Referring to the photo (page 10) as a guide, appliqué a leaf approximately 1½" from each stem end. Appliqué a ladybug body onto the center of each stem piece, and then appliqué a head to each body.

Make the Dimensional Flowers

1. Trace the flower petal and flower center patterns on page 14 onto template plastic and cut them out.

2. Using the petal template and the water-soluble pen, trace 40 petals onto the wrong side of the remaining red check. Cut out the petals on the marked lines.

3. Place two flower petals right sides together. Beginning and ending with a backstitch, sew ¼" from the curved edges, leaving the straight edge open. Trim the seam allowances to approximately ⅛". Turn the petal to the right side and press. Repeat to make a total of 20 petals.

4. Thread the embroidery needle with three strands of white floss and knot one end. Baste along the bottom edge of five petals, stitching one right after another without cutting the floss.

5. Pull the floss strands to gather the petals, and then bring the two end petals tightly together to form a circle. Knot the floss ends to secure the flower shape. Repeat with the remaining petals to make a total of four petal units.

6. Place a completed petal unit over each stem intersection. Machine sew directly on top of the gathers around the entire center of each petal unit.

7. Using the flower-center template and the water-soluble pen, trace four circles onto the wrong side of the yellow square. Cut out the circles on the marked lines.

8. Turn under and finger-press approximately ¼" around a yellow circle to create a hem. Thread the embroidery needle with three strands of yellow floss and knot one end. Baste approximately ⅛" from the folded edge around the entire circle. Unthread the needle and leave the excess tail loose. Do not gather the edges yet! Repeat with the remaining flower-center circles.

9. Place a basted center circle right side down over the center of each petal unit. Machine stitch a circle, slightly larger than the circle stitched over the petals in step 6, through the flower center and petal units, backstitching at the beginning and end of the stitching.

10. To finish each flower center, pull the loose end of the embroidery floss to gather the edges of the center circle tightly. Thread the end of the floss back through the needle and pull the floss through the flower center to the wrong side of the white background square. Pull tightly, and then knot the thread on the back of the background square.

Assemble the Quilt Top

Use ¼"-wide seam allowances and sew with right sides together.

1. Center and sew red-print triangles to opposite sides of the appliquéd background square. Press the seam allowances toward the triangles. Repeat on the opposite sides of the square. The quilt top should measure 24½" x 24½".

2. Refer to the quilt assembly diagram below to sew the black 2" x 24½" inner-border strips to the sides of the quilt center. Press the seam allowances toward the strips. Sew the black 2" x 27½" inner-border strips to the top and bottom of the quilt center. Press the seam allowances toward the strips.

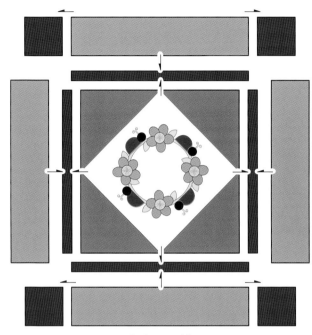

Quilt assembly

3. Join red-checked 6½" x 27½" outer-border strips to the sides of the quilt top. Press the seam allowances toward the inner border. Sew black 6½" squares to both ends of each of the remaining red-checked 6½" x 27½" strips. Press the seam allowances toward the squares. Join these strips to the top and bottom of the quilt top. Press the seam allowances toward the inner border.

Finish the Quilt

1. Using the embroidery pattern below, trace one pair of antennae onto the head of each ladybug. Backstitch (page 8) the lines with three strands of black embroidery floss and the embroidery needle.

Antennae embroidery pattern

2. Refer to "Finishing Your Quilts" (page 8) to layer the quilt top with batting and backing; baste the layers together.

3. Bind the quilt with the black 2½"-wide strips.

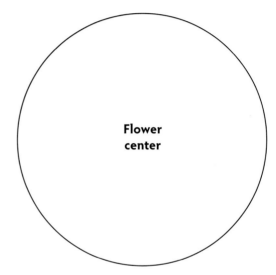

¼" seam allowance

Flower petal

Leave open.

Flower center

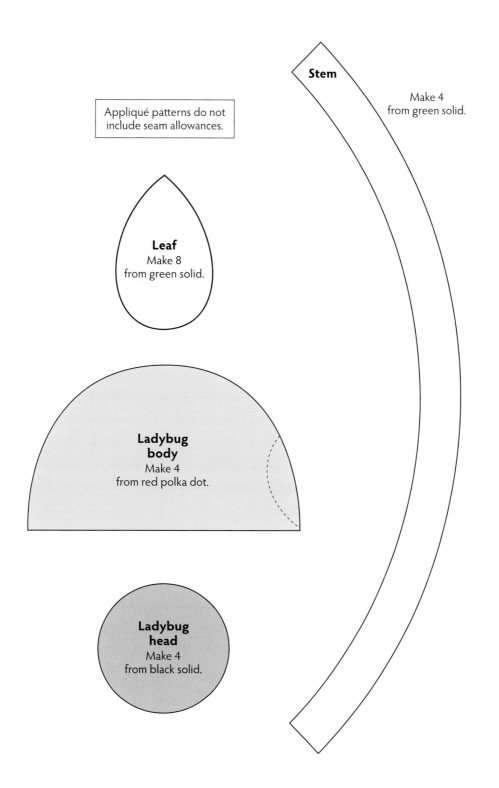

Appliqué patterns do not include seam allowances.

Stem

Make 4 from green solid.

Leaf
Make 8 from green solid.

Ladybug body
Make 4 from red polka dot.

Ladybug head
Make 4 from black solid.

Anchors Aweigh!

Finished quilt: 43" x 43"

Pieced by Kristin Roylance; machine quilted by Molly Kohler

This fun quilt is perfect for the little sailor in your life. The four boats come complete with three-dimensional flags flying high above the ships. The soft chenille waves will have your little sea captain ready to set sail for high adventure!

Materials

Yardage is based on 42"-wide fabric.

¼ yard *each* of 10 assorted cream, blue, and brown small-scale prints for quilt center (use the boat, sail, and corner-triangle fabrics in this assortment if desired)

¾ yard of light-blue solid for corner triangles

½ yard of medium-blue chenille fabric for waves (you'll need ½ yard no matter what the fabric width is)

½ yard of cream small-scale print for sails

¼ yard of brown tone on tone for boats

4" x 9" rectangle of red check for flags

½ yard of brown solid for binding

2⅞ yards of fabric for backing

51" x 51" piece of batting

4 yards of brown medium rickrack

1 yard of brown baby rickrack

Template plastic

Water-soluble pen

Cutting

From *each* of the 10 assorted prints, cut:
1 strip, 3½" x 42"; crosscut into 10 squares, 3½" x 3½" (100 total)

From the cream small-scale print, cut:
1 strip, 6½" x 42"; crosscut into 4 squares, 6½" x 6½"
1 strip, 5" x 42"; crosscut into 4 squares, 5" x 5"

From the light-blue solid, cut:
2 squares, 14" x 14"; cut into quarters diagonally to make 8 large triangles
2 squares, 5½" x 5½"; cut into quarters diagonally to make 8 small triangles
4 strips, 2" x 42"; crosscut into:
  • 4 pieces, 2" x 18½"
  • 8 rectangles, 2" x 4¼"
  • 8 squares, 2" x 2"

From the blue chenille fabric, cut:
4 strips, 3½" x 42"

From the brown tone on tone, cut:
2 strips, 2" x 42"; crosscut into 4 pieces, 2" x 11"

From the brown solid, cut:
5 strips, 2½" x 42"

Assemble the Quilt Top

Use ¼"-wide seam allowances and sew with right sides together unless otherwise stated.

① Lay out the assorted 3½" squares into 10 rows of 10 squares each. Sew the squares in each row together. Press the seam allowances open. Sew the rows together. Press the seam allowances open. Square up the quilt center to 30½" x 30½".

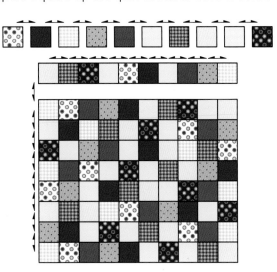

② Fold each of the cream 5" and 6½" squares in half diagonally, wrong sides together, to make the sail pieces; press.

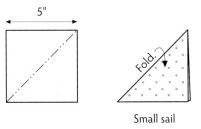

Small sail

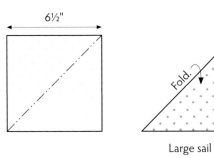

Large sail

③ Lay a large sail triangle on top of a large light-blue triangle as shown with the 90° angles aligned. Baste the sail in place ⅛" from the outer edges. Repeat to make a total of four large sail units.

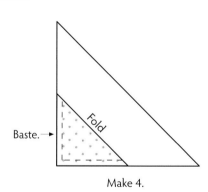

Make 4.

④ Lay a small sail triangle on top of a large light-blue triangle as shown with the 90° angles aligned. Baste the sail in place ⅛" from the outer edges. Repeat to make a total of four small sail units.

Make 4.

⑤ Trace the flag pattern (page 21) onto template plastic and cut it out. Fold the red 4" x 9" rectangle in half, right sides together as shown above right. Using the flag template and the water-soluble pen, trace four flags onto the wrong side of one half of the red square, leaving ½" between shapes. Stitch directly on the lines of each

triangle, leaving the short bottom edge open and backstitching at the beginning and end of the stitching line.

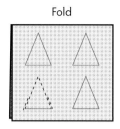

Fold

⑥ Cut out each flag ⅛" from the stitching lines. Trim across the seam allowances at the tip of each flag. Turn each flag to the right side; press. Topstitch along the long edges of each flag.

← Trim.

Topstitch long edges.

⑦ Baste a flag directly above each small sail from step 4 as shown.

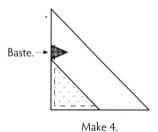

Baste. →

Make 4.

⑧ Sew a large sail triangle from step 3 to each small sail triangle from step 7 as shown. Press the seam allowances toward the large sail.

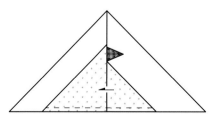

9. Center and sew a light-blue 2" x 18½" strip to the bottom of each sail unit. Press the seam allowances away from the sail units.

10. Cut the baby rickrack into four 9" lengths. Fold under one end of one length approximately ¼". Using matching thread, position the rickrack on the center seam of a sail unit, with the folded end ¼" above the top of the red flag; stitch in place. Repeat with the remaining sail sections.

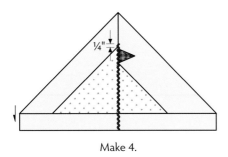

Make 4.

11. Draw a diagonal line on the wrong side of each light-blue 2" square. Place a marked square on the right end of a brown tone-on-tone 2" x 11" piece as shown, right sides together and aligning the raw edges. Sew directly on the drawn line. Fold the square over to meet at the bottom-right corner; press. Repeat on the opposite end, orienting the drawn line as shown.

Make 4.

12. Sew light-blue 2" x 4¼" rectangles to both ends of each unit from step 11 to make four boat units. Press the seam allowances toward the rectangles.

Make 4.

13. Join a sail section from step 10 to each of the boat units from step 12. Press the seam allowances toward the boat sections. Sew small light-blue triangles to both straight sides of each unit. Press the seam allowances toward the triangles.

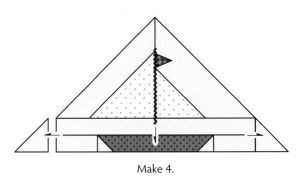

Make 4.

14. Refer to the quilt assembly diagram on page 21 to center and sew a chenille strip to the bottom of each boat unit. Press the seam allowances toward the boat sections. Trim the chenille strip even with the diagonal sides of the sail-boat unit.

15. Center and sew sailboat units to opposite sides of the pieced center square. The triangle ends will extend past the pieced center slightly. Repeat on the remaining sides.

16. Cut the medium rickrack into four 36" lengths. Center a length over each seam between the chenille strip and pieced center and stitch it in place with matching thread. Trim the excess fabric and rickrack at the pieced center points even with the edges of the quilt top.

Finish the Quilt

1. Refer to "Finishing Your Quilts" (page 8) to layer the quilt top with batting and backing; baste the layers together.

2. Bind the quilt with the brown-solid 2½"-wide strips.

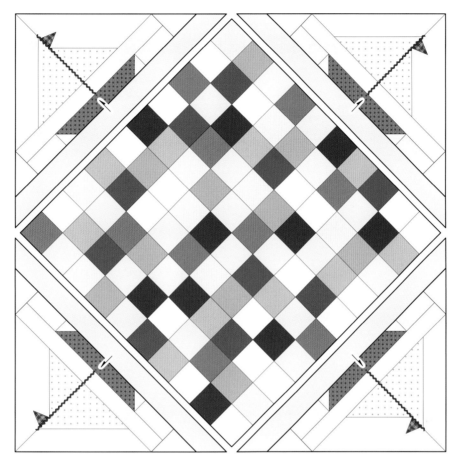

Quilt assembly

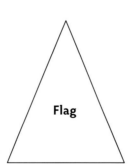

Flag

Butterfly Kisses

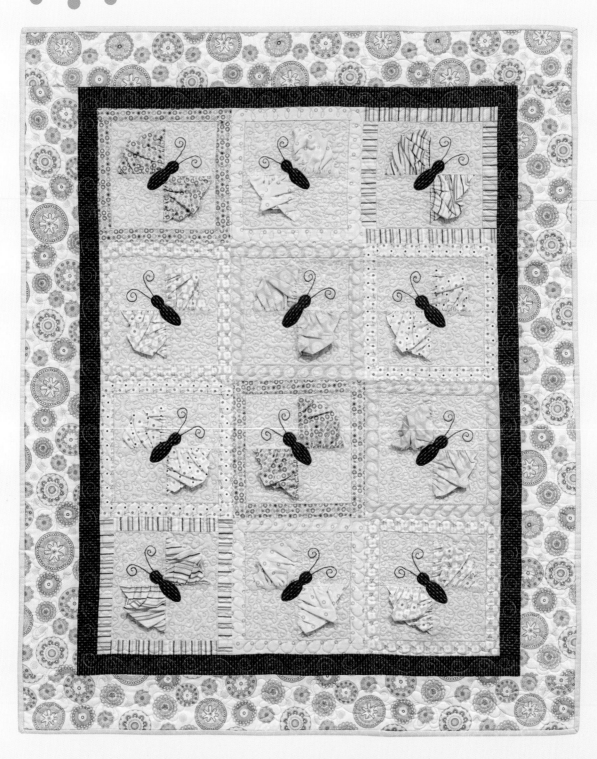

Finished quilt: 41½" x 51½" • **Finished block:** 10" x 10"

Pieced by Kristin Roylance; machine quilted by Molly Kohler

This sweet quilt will have your favorite little girl floating off to sleep with flying dimensional butterflies. Sweet dreams!

Materials

Yardage is based on 42"-wide fabric.

⅜ yard *each* of 6 assorted pastel prints and stripes for butterfly wings and block frames

1⅓ yards of blue tone on tone for background and binding

¾ yard of light print for outer border

⅓ yard of brown solid for butterfly bodies and inner border

2¾ yards of fabric for backing

50" x 60" piece of batting

⅛ yard of 17"-wide paper-backed fusible web

Brown embroidery floss

Size 5 embroidery needle

Water-soluble pen

Cutting

From the blue tone on tone, cut:

6 strips, 4½" x 42"; crosscut into 48 squares, 4½" x 4½"

5 strips, 2½" x 42"

From *each* of the 6 assorted pastel prints and stripes, cut:

1 strip, 6" x 42"; crosscut into 4 squares, 6" x 6" (24 total)

3 strips, 1½" x 42"; crosscut into:
- 4 pieces, 1½" x 10½" (24 total)
- 4 pieces, 1½" x 8½" (24 total)

From the brown solid, cut:

2 strips, 2" x 33½"

2 strips, 2" x 40½"

From the light print, cut:

5 strips, 4½" x 42"

Make the Butterfly Blocks

Use ¼"-wide seam allowances and sew with right sides together.

1. Fold each assorted print and stripe 6" square in half diagonally, wrong sides together; press.

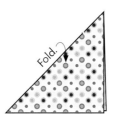

2. Hand or machine baste ⅛" from the raw edges of each folded triangle, leaving long tails at both ends. Pull the threads from each end until both gathered edges of the triangle measure 3½"; secure the ends.

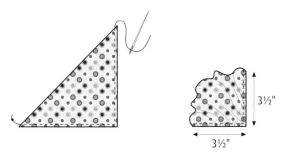

3. Baste a "wing" triangle from step 2 onto one corner of a blue 4½" square, making sure the corners are aligned. Repeat to make a total of 24 wing squares.

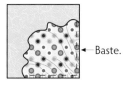

Make 24.

4. Sew each wing square to one of the remaining blue 4½" squares. Press the seam allowances toward the blue fabric.

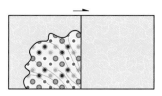

Make 24.

5. Sew two matching wing units together so that the wings are opposite one another as shown. Press the seam allowances open. Repeat to make a total of 12 butterfly units.

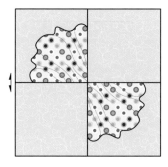

Make 12.

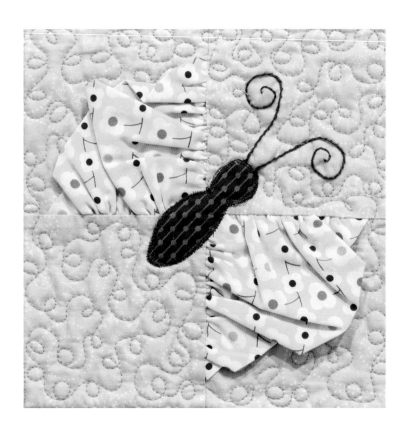

6. Sew assorted 1½" x 8½" pieces that match the wings to the sides of each butterfly unit. Press the seam allowances toward the frame pieces. Add the matching 1½" x 10½" pieces to the top and bottom of each unit to complete the blocks. Press the seam allowances toward the frame pieces.

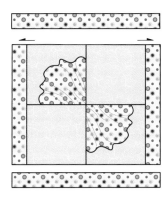

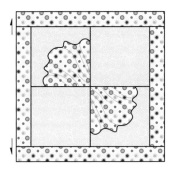

Make 12.

7. Refer to "Fusible-Web Appliqué" (page 7) and use the pattern (page 26) to prepare the appliqués from the remaining brown fabric. Appliqué a body between the wings on each block.

8. Using the water-soluble pen and the pattern (page 26), trace one pair of antennae onto the head of each butterfly. Backstitch (page 8) the lines with three strands of brown embroidery floss and the embroidery needle.

Assemble the Quilt Top

1. Refer to the quilt assembly diagram at right to lay out the blocks in four rows of three blocks each. Pay attention to the direction the butterflies are facing. They should all be facing upward in alternate directions within each row and from row to row.

2. Sew the blocks in each row together. Press the seam allowances open. Sew the rows together. Press the seam allowances open. Square up the quilt top to 30½" x 40½".

3. Sew the brown 2" x 40½" inner-border strips to the sides of the quilt top. Press the seam allowances toward the border strips. Sew the brown 2" x 33½" inner-border strips to the top and bottom of the quilt top. Press the seam allowances toward the border strips.

4. Sew the light-print 4½" x 42" outer-border strips together end to end to make one long strip. Press the seam allowances in one direction. From the pieced strip, cut two strips, 4½" x 43½". Sew these strips to the sides of the quilt top. Press the seam allowances toward the inner border. From the remainder of the pieced strip, cut two strips, 4½" x 41½". Sew these strips to the top and bottom of the quilt top. Press the seam allowances toward the inner border.

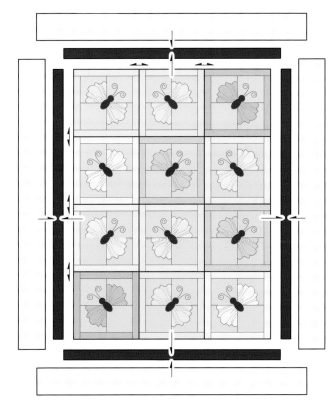

Quilt assembly

Finish the Quilt

1. Refer to "Finishing Your Quilts" (page 8) to layer the quilt top with batting and backing; baste the layers together.

2. Bind the quilt with the blue 2½"-wide strips.

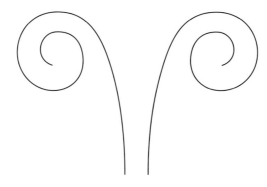

Butterfly antennae embroidery pattern

Butterfly body
Make 12 from brown solid.

Appliqué pattern does not include seam allowance.

Are We There Yet?

Finished quilt: 36" x 45"

Pieced by Kristin Roylance; machine quilted by Molly Kohler

With zigzag roads, a rickrack racing track, and a stop-sign pocket to safely store toy cars, this fun activity quilt will have both little ones and adults smiling! Your little driver may even forget to ask, "Are we there yet?"

Materials

Yardage is based on 42"-wide fabric.

⅛ yard *each* of 10 assorted red, brown, and blue prints for zigzag strips

1¼ yards of white-on-white print for zigzag strips, middle border, and sign-letter appliqués

⅔ yard of brown print for inner and outer borders

¼ yard of red print for car and stop-sign appliqués (can be one of the same prints used for the zigzag strips)

10" x 10" square of blue print for go-sign and car-window appliqués (can be one of the same prints used for the zigzag strips)

6" x 12" piece of black solid for wheel appliqués

3" x 8" piece of brown print for car-bumper appliqués (can be one of the same prints used for the zigzag strips)

½ yard of blue print for binding (can be one of the same prints used for the zigzag strip)

3 yards of fabric for backing

44" x 53" piece of batting

1 yard of Pellon fusible, nonwoven 1" Quilter's Grid On Point

Washable-glue stick

4½ yards of blue medium rickrack for track

8 white 1"-diameter buttons for wheels

Template plastic

1½" of ¾"-wide sew-on Velcro

Cutting

From the white-on-white print, cut:

4 strips, 4" x 42"

11 strips, 1½" x 42"; crosscut *1 of the strips* into 10 rectangles, 1½" x 2½"

2 strips, 2½" x 42"; crosscut into 19 squares, 2½" x 2½". Cut each square in half diagonally to make 38 large triangles. Cut *1* triangle in half to make 2 small triangles.

From *each* of the 10 assorted red, brown, and blue prints, cut:

1 strip, 1½" x 42" (10 total)

1 rectangle, 1½" x 2½" (10 total)

From the brown print, cut:

4 strips, 2" x 42"

4 strips, 3" x 42"

From the blue print, cut:

5 strips, 2½" x 42"

Piece the Quilt Center

Use ¼"-wide seam allowances and sew with right sides together.

1. Using the 1½" x 42" strips, sew each white strip to a red, brown, or blue strip along the long edges to make a total of 10 strip sets. Press the seam allowances toward the colored strips. Crosscut each strip set into 16 segments, 2½" wide.

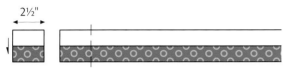

Make 10 strip sets.
Cut 16 segments from each.

2. Using the 1½" x 2½" rectangles, sew each white rectangle to a red, brown, or blue rectangle along the long edges. Make a total of 10 pieced squares. Press the seam allowances toward the colored rectangles.

Make 10.

3. Stack the pieced squares from steps 1 and 2 into groups by fabric. You should have 17 squares in each group. Arrange the squares from one group right side up on the fusible side of the Quilter's Grid as shown so the print creates a zig-zag pattern across the web. Fuse the squares in place, following the manufacturer's instructions.

4. Repeat step 3 with the remaining groups of squares to create a total of 10 zigzag rows. Fuse the large white triangles to the empty spaces

along the edges of the quilt center. Fuse the small white triangles to the upper corners.

⑤ Beginning at the upper-left corner, fold the first diagonal row on top of the second diagonal row, right sides together. The fold will be exactly where the two diagonal rows come together. Stitch ¼" from the folded edge. Repeat with all the parallel diagonal rows.

⑥ From the back of the grid, make snips ¼" into the seam where the squares intersect. Lightly press the seam allowances in opposite directions as they naturally fall.

⑦ Beginning at the upper-right corner, sew the remaining rows in the same manner as you did in step 6.

⑧ Lightly press the finished quilt center from the right side. The seams will naturally fall in the correct directions.

⑨ Using a ruler and rotary cutter, even up the edges of the quilt top, cutting directly through the center of the rectangle points as indicated by the dashed lines.

Add the Borders

① Measure the length of the quilt top through the center. Trim two brown 2" x 42" inner-border strips to the length measured. Sew these strips to the sides of the quilt top. Press the seam allowances toward the border strips.

② Measure the width of the quilt top through the center, including the border strips just added. Trim the remaining two brown 2" x 42" inner-border strips to the length measured. Sew these strips to the top and bottom of the quilt top. Press the seam allowances toward the border strips.

③ Repeat steps 1 and 2 with the white 4"-wide middle-border strips, pressing the seam allowances toward the inner border.

④ Repeat steps 1 and 2 with the brown 3"-wide outer-border strips, pressing the seam allowances toward the outer border.

Appliqué the Quilt Top

① Using the washable-glue stick, adhere the rick-rack to the middle border to create a racetrack, referring to the photo (page 27) as needed for placement. Start the rickrack 23" from the top of the quilt and end the rickrack 15" from the bottom of the quilt. There will be a space approximately 6" long between the ends of the rickrack. Use a narrow zigzag stitch to sew through the middle of the rickrack to secure it to the quilt top.

② Refer to "Fusible-Web Appliqué" (page 7) and use the patterns (pages 32 and 33) to prepare the car, go-sign, and stop-sign-bottom appliqués from the fabrics indicated.

③ Using the photo as a guide, appliqué the prepared car pieces to the quilt center in the order indicated on the patterns.

④ Using the prepared letters, appliqué *GO* to the center of the blue circle. Appliqué the go sign to the beginning of the rickrack racetrack and the stop-sign bottom onto the end of the rickrack racetrack, centering the ends of the rickrack under the signs. Stitch the hook portion of the Velcro across the bottom edge of the stop-sign appliqué.

⑤ Trace the stop-sign-top pattern (page 32) onto template plastic and cut it out. Using the water-soluble pen and the template, trace two stop signs onto the wrong side of the remainder of the red print. Sew the pieces together around the outer edges. Cut a 2" slit in the middle of one layer of the stop-sign pieces and turn the sign to the right side. Hand stitch the opening closed, making sure your stitches do not go through to the other side; press.

⑥ Using the prepared letters, appliqué *STOP* to the center of the stop-sign top on the side that wasn't slit. Stitch the loop portion of the Velcro to the wrong side of the sign across the bottom edge. Position the sign over the appliquéd stop-sign bottom, aligning the edges. Leaving the bottom three edges unstitched, appliqué the sign in place.

Finish the Quilt

① Sew a button to the center of each wheel.
Note: If this quilt is for a baby or very young child, you may want to appliqué white circles onto the wheels instead of using buttons, to prevent a choking hazard.

② Refer to "Finishing Your Quilts" (page 8) to layer the quilt top with batting and backing; baste the layers together.

③ Bind the quilt with the blue 2½"-wide strips.

Appliqué patterns do not include seam allowances.

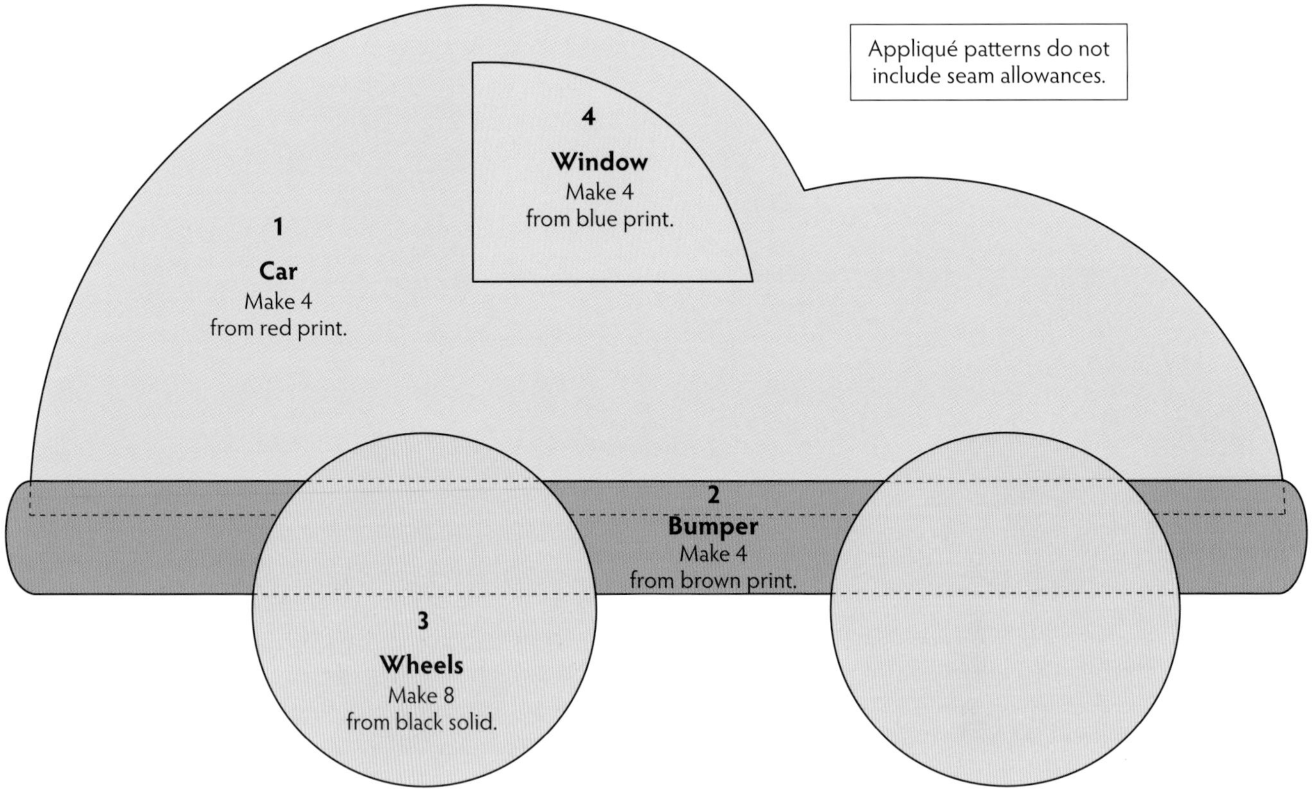

4

Window

Make 4 from blue print.

1

Car

Make 4 from red print.

2

Bumper

Make 4 from brown print.

3

Wheels

Make 8 from black solid.

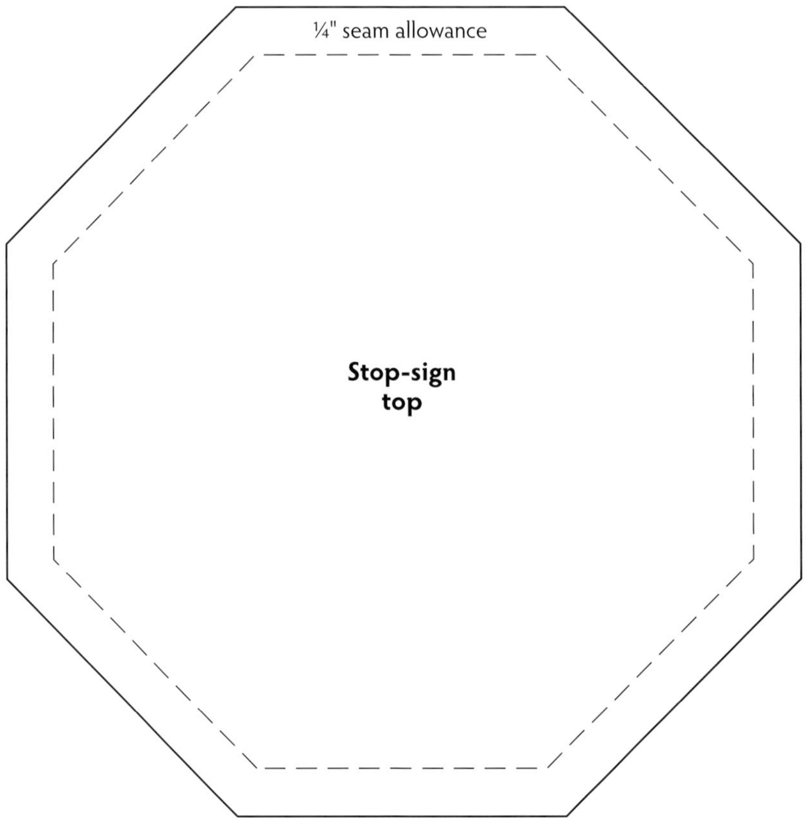

¼" seam allowance

Stop-sign top

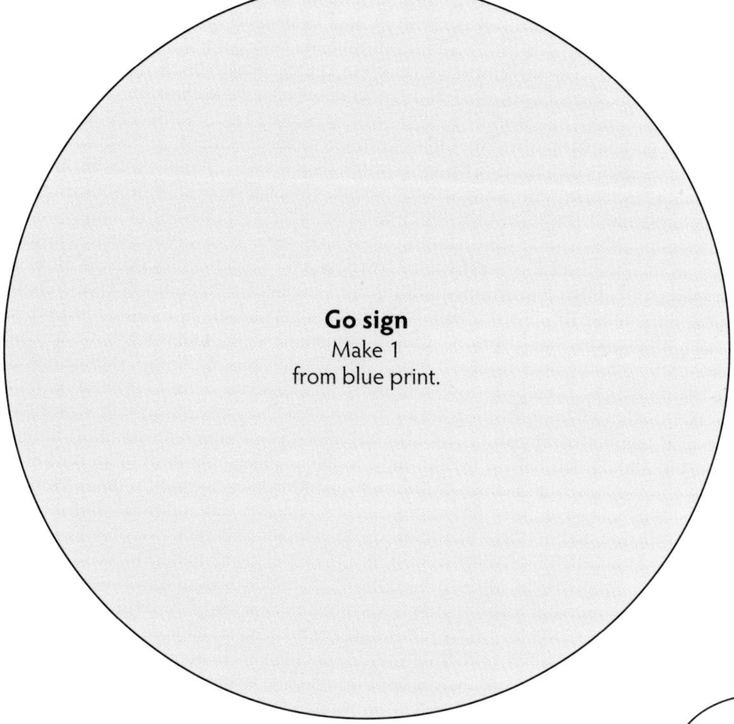

Go sign
Make 1
from blue print.

Appliqué patterns do not
include seam allowances.

Cut 1 set of letters
for each word from white print.

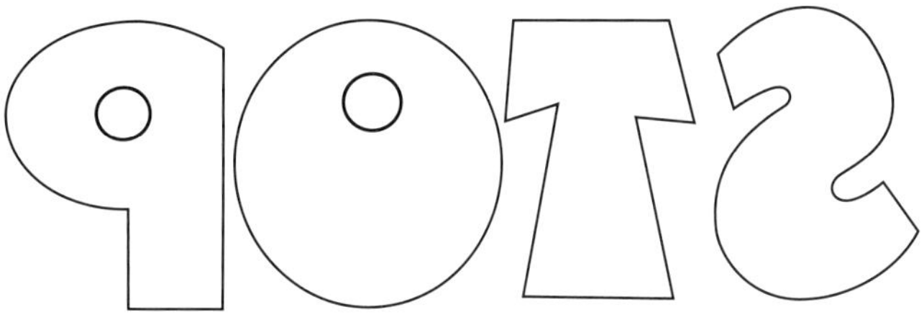

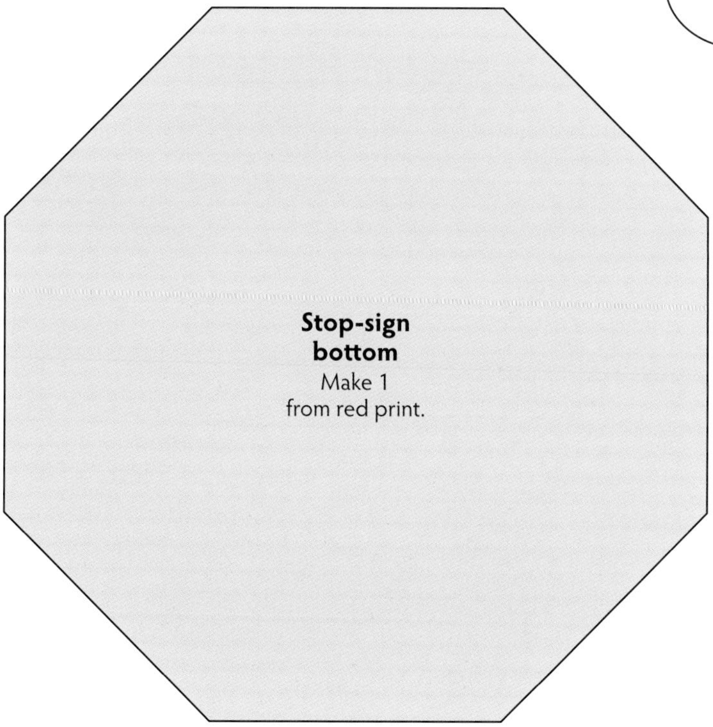

**Stop-sign
bottom**
Make 1
from red print.

You Are My Sunshine

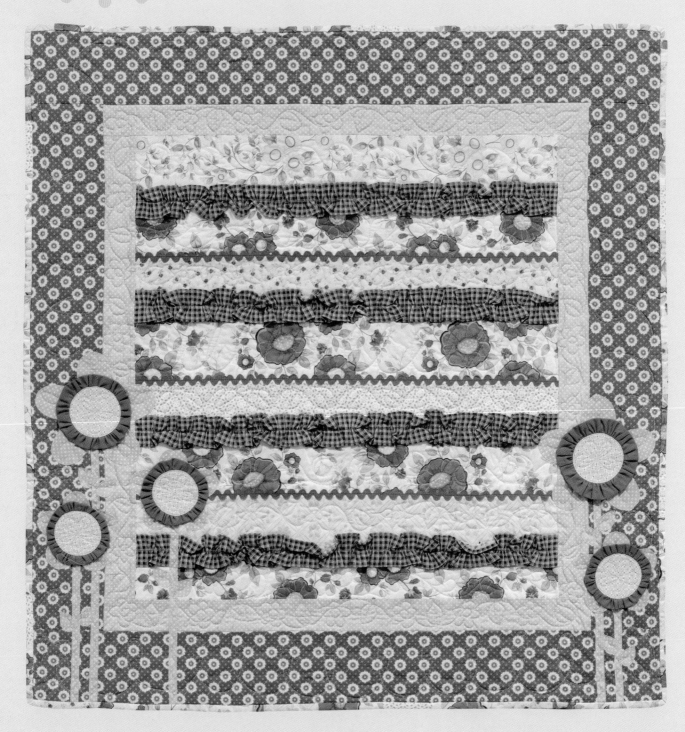

Finished quilt: 40" x 42"

Pieced by Kristin Roylance; machine quilted by Molly Kohler

This adorable quilt is filled with ruffles and blooming flowers. It will brighten even the gloomiest of days!

Materials

Yardage is based on 42"-wide fabric.

¾ yard of large-scale coral floral for pieced center and binding

⅔ yard of dark-coral floral for outer border

⅓ yard *each* of 2 medium-scale florals for pieced center and binding

½ yard of dark-coral plaid for ruffle strips

¼ yard *each* of 2 small-scale florals for pieced center and binding

⅜ yard of light-green tone on tone for inner border and flower stems

⅜ yard of dark-coral solid for flower ruffles

⅛ yard of light-coral print for flower petals

⅛ yard of light-yellow print for flower centers

2⅔ yards of fabric for backing

2½ yards of green medium rickrack

48" x 50" piece of batting

½ yard of 17"-wide paper-backed fusible web

Cutting

From the large-scale coral floral, cut:

2 strips, 5" x 42"; crosscut *1 of the strips* into:
- 1 rectangle, 5" x 10"
- 1 piece, 4½" x 10"
- 1 piece, 4" x 10"
- 1 piece, 3½" x 10"

1 strip, 4½" x 42"

1 strip, 4" x 42"

1 strip, 3½" x 42"

From 1 of the medium-scale florals, cut:

1 strip, 4½" x 42"

1 piece, 4½" x 10"

From the remaining medium-scale floral, cut:

1 strip, 4" x 42"

1 piece, 4" x 10"

From *each* of the 2 small-scale florals, cut:

1 strip, 3½" x 42" (2 total)

1 piece, 3½" x 10" (2 total)

From the light-green tone on tone, cut:

2 strips, 2½" x 29"

2 strips, 2½" x 31"

1 piece, 3" x 18"

From the dark-coral plaid, cut:

4 strips, 3" x 42"

From the dark-coral floral, cut:

2 strips, 5" x 33"

2 strips, 5" x 40"

From the dark-coral solid, cut:

5 strips, 2" x 21"

From the paper-backed fusible web, cut:

1 piece, 3" x 18"

Piece the Quilt Center

Use ¼"-wide seam allowances and sew with right sides together.

1. Sew the floral 42"-long strips together along the long edges in the order shown on page 36 to make a strip set. Press the seam allowances open. Crosscut the strip set into one piece, 27" wide, for the quilt top, and five segments, 2½" wide, for the scrappy binding. Set the

binding strips aside. Square up the quilt-center piece to 27" x 29", if necessary.

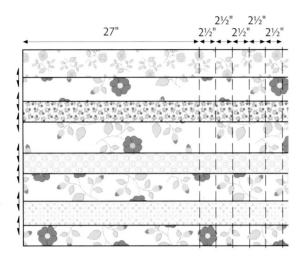

Make 1 strip set.
Cut 1 segment, 27" wide, and 5 segments, 2½" wide.

② Sew the floral 10"-long pieces together in the same order as you did in step 1 to make a strip set. Crosscut the strip set into one strip, 2½" wide, for the scrappy binding. Set it aside with the other binding strips.

③ Prepare the ruffle strips by pressing under ¼" twice along both long edges of each dark-coral plaid 3" x 42" strip. Use a zigzag stitch to secure the turned-under edges. Press each strip in half lengthwise, wrong sides together. Open up the strips. Hand or machine baste along the crease of each strip, leaving long thread tails at the beginning and end. Pull the thread tails to gather each strip to approximately 29". Evenly adjust the gathers.

Pull thread until strip is 29" long.

④ Position a gathered ruffle strip on the first, third, fifth, and seventh seam lines of the pieced quilt top, leaving approximately 1" of ruffle extending beyond the quilt top at both ends. Stitch the ruffle strips in place through the center of each strip.

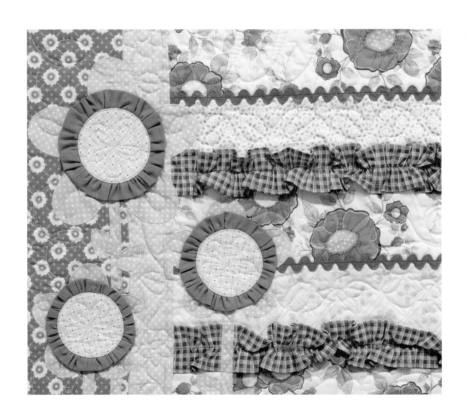

5 Cut the rickrack into three 30" lengths. Center a length on the second, fourth, and sixth seams of the quilt top, leaving approximately 1½" of rickrack extending beyond the quilt top at both ends. Stitch the rickrack in place through the center of each length.

Add the Borders

1 Sew the light-green 2½" x 29" inner-border strips to the sides of the quilt top. Press the seam allowances toward the border strips. Trim the excess ruffle and rickrack ends even with the seam allowances. Sew the light-green 2½" x 31" inner-border strips to the top and bottom of the quilt top. Press the seam allowances toward the border strips.

2 Sew the dark-coral floral 5" x 33" outer-border strips to the sides of the quilt top. Press the seam allowances toward the outer-border strips. Sew the dark-coral floral 5" x 40" outer-border strips to the top and bottom of the quilt top. Press the seam allowances toward the outer-border strips.

Appliqué the Quilt Top

1 Follow the manufacturer's instructions to apply the 3" x 18" piece of fusible web to the light-green 3" x 18" piece. From the prepared piece, cut five ½"-wide strips. Trim the strips to the following lengths for the flower stems: 18", 15½", 13", 11", and 8".

2 Refer to the stem placement diagram below and "Fusible-Web Appliqué" (page 7) to appliqué the stems to the quilt top.

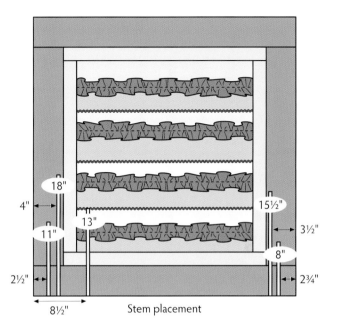

Stem placement

3 Refer to "Fusible-Web Appliqué" and use the patterns (page 39) to prepare the remaining appliqués from the fabrics indicated.

4 Appliqué two leaves on each stem, using the quilt photo as a guide for placement. Appliqué five small flower petals to the top of the 11", 13", and 8" stems, making sure the stem end is centered between the bottom two petals. Appliqué five large flower petals to the top of the 18" and 15½" stems in the same manner.

5. Sew the short ends of the dark-coral solid 2" x 21" strips right sides together to make a ring. Press the seam allowances open. Fold each circle in half, wrong sides together. Hand or machine baste ¼" from the raw edges, leaving long thread tails at each end.

6. Pull on the thread ends to gather two of the rings so they measure 2½" in diameter; secure the thread ends. Gather the remaining three rings so they measure approximately 2¼" in diameter; secure the thread ends.

7. Place the 2½" ruffled rings directly on top of the large flowers, being sure to cover all the straight edges of the flower petals. Using a straight stitch, sew directly on top of the gathers to secure the ruffles to the flowers. Repeat to sew the 2¼" ruffled rings to the small flower petals.

8. Appliqué the large flower centers to the center of each large flower, and the small flower centers to the center of the small flowers.

Finish the Quilt

1. Refer to "Finishing Your Quilts" (page 8) to layer the quilt top with batting and backing; baste the layers together.

2. Sew the pieced binding strips that you set aside earlier together end to end to make one long strip. Bind the quilt with the pieced strip.

**Large
flower petal**
Make 10
from light-coral print.

Appliqué patterns do not
include seam allowances.

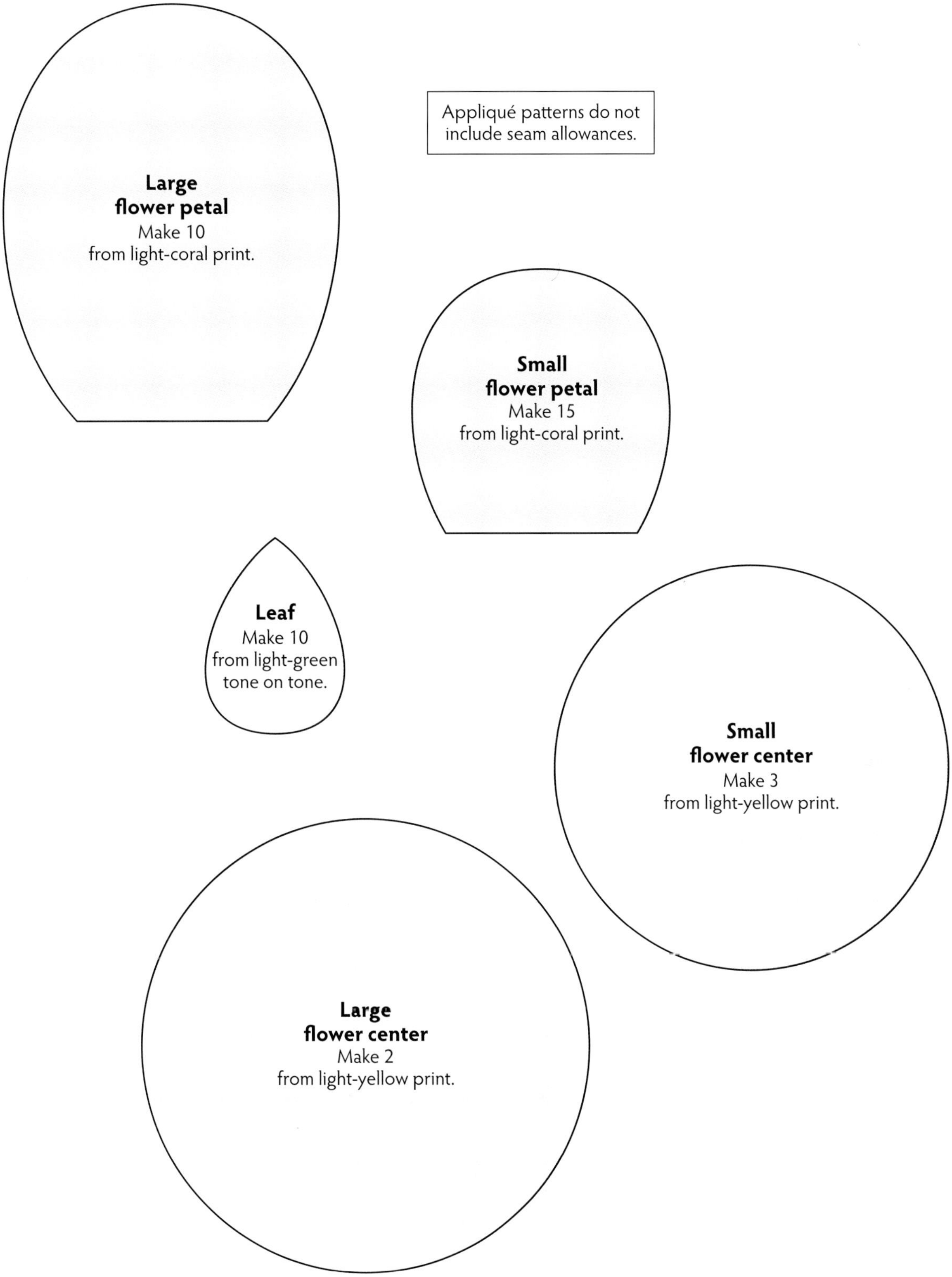

**Small
flower petal**
Make 15
from light-coral print.

Leaf
Make 10
from light-green
tone on tone.

**Small
flower center**
Make 3
from light-yellow print.

**Large
flower center**
Make 2
from light-yellow print.

Rodeo Roundup

Finished quilt: 42½" x 52½"

Pieced by Kristin Roylance; machine quilted by Molly Kohler

This adorable rodeo quilt features a bandanna, boots, and of course a cowboy—or cowgirl—hat. You can rope this quilt together in no time flat!

• • •

Materials

Yardage is based on 42"-wide fabric.

¼ yard *each* of 10 assorted small-scale cowboy-themed prints for pieced rows

⅞ yard of red print for plain rows*

⅔ yard of beige solid for hat, boots, and bandanna background

⅝ yard of medium-brown print for boots and binding

½ yard of beige print for star background**

¼ yard of blue bandanna print for star appliqués and bandanna

¼ yard of dark-brown polka dot for hat

5" x 5" square of black solid for boot heels

2¾ yards of fabric for backing

50" x 60" piece of batting

2½ yards of brown jumbo rickrack

7¼ yards of brown medium rickrack

¼ yard of 17"-wide paper-backed fusible web

Template plastic

Water-soluble pen

If your fabric measures at least 42½" wide after removing the selvages, you'll need only ½ yard of fabric.

**If your fabric measures at least 42½" wide after removing the selvages, you'll need only ¼ yard of fabric.*

Cutting

From *each* of the assorted cowboy prints, cut:

2 strips, 2" x 42"; crosscut into 34 squares, 2" x 2" (340 total)

From the beige solid, cut:

2 strips, 8½" x 42"; crosscut into:
- 2 pieces, 6" x 8½"
- 3 pieces, 2½" x 8½"

1 square, 4⅞" x 4⅞"

2 squares, 2⅞" x 2⅞"

4 rectangles, 2½" x 4½"

2 strips, 1½" x 42"; crosscut into:
- 3 pieces, 1½" x 8½"
- 2 pieces, 1½" x 5½"
- 1 piece, 1½" x 4½"
- 2 pieces, 1½" x 3½"
- 16 squares, 1½" x 1½"
- 2 squares, ½" x ½"

From the dark-brown polka dot, cut:

1 piece, 3½" x 4½"

1 square, 2⅞" x 2⅞"

1 piece, 1½" x 8½"

2 pieces, 1½" x 2½"

From the blue bandanna print, cut:

1 square, 4⅞" x 4⅞"

1 piece, 4" x 12"

1 piece, 1½" x 8½"

1 piece, 1½" x 4½"

From the medium-brown print, cut:

5 strips, 2½" x 42"

2 pieces, 3½" x 5½"

1 square, 2⅞" x 2⅞"

2 pieces, 1½" x 4½"

From the black solid, cut:

2 squares, 1½" x 1½"

Continued on page 42

Continued from page 41

From the red print, cut:
2 strips, 7" x 42"*
3 strips, 3½" x 42"*

From the beige print, cut:
2 strips, 7" x 42"*

If your fabric measures at least 42½" wide after trimming off the selvages, you'll need only 1 red strip, 7" x 42½"; 2 red strips, 3½" x 42½"; and 1 beige strip, 7" x 42½".

Assemble the Scrappy-Squares Rows

Use ¼"-wide seam allowances and sew with right sides together.

1. Randomly sew 28 assorted cowboy-print 2" squares together side by side to make a strip. Press the seam allowances open. Repeat to make a total of 12 strips. You'll have four squares left over for another project.

2. Sew three strips together along the long edges to make a row. Press the seam allowances open. Repeat to make a total of four sections.

Make 4 sections.

Fast Fusible
An alternate method for assembling the rows would be to use Pellon fusible, non-woven 1" Quilter's Grid. Follow the manufacturer's instructions to make the four sections using 84 squares for each section. You'll need 1½ yards of fusible grid to make the four sections.

Make the Cowboy-Hat Unit

1. Draw a diagonal line from corner to corner on the wrong side of a beige-solid 2⅞" square. Layer the marked square on top of the dark-brown 2⅞" square, aligning the edges. Sew ¼" from both sides of the drawn line. Cut directly on the marked line to make two half-square-triangle units. Press the seam allowances toward the dark-brown fabric.

Make 2.

(2) Sew a beige-solid 2½" x 4½" piece to each half-square-triangle unit from step 1 as shown. Press the seam allowances toward the rectangles.

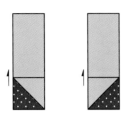

(3) Draw a diagonal line from corner to corner on the wrong side of four beige-solid 1½" squares.

(4) Place a marked square from step 3 on the left end of a dark-brown 1½" x 2½" piece with the marked line oriented as shown. Sew on the marked line. Press the square up toward the top-left corner. Place another marked square on the right end of the rectangle, orienting the marked line as shown. Sew on the marked line. Press the square up toward the top-right corner. Repeat to make a total of two units.

Make 2.

(5) Sew the two units from step 4 together along the short ends. Press the seam allowances open.

(6) Sew the beige-solid 1½" x 4½" piece to the top of the unit from step 5. Sew the dark-brown 3½" x 4½" piece to the bottom of the unit. Add the blue 1½" x 4½" piece to the bottom of this unit. Press the seam allowances open.

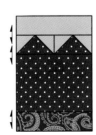

(7) Sew the units from step 2 to the sides of the unit from step 6. Press the seam allowances open.

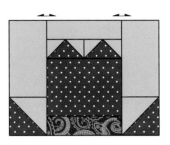

(8) Draw a diagonal line from corner to corner on the wrong side of two beige-solid 1½" squares. Place a marked square on the left end of the dark-brown 1½" x 8½" piece with the marked line oriented as shown. Sew on the marked line. Press the square down toward the bottom-left corner. Place the remaining marked square on the right end of the rectangle, orienting the marked line as shown. Sew on the marked line. Press the square down toward the bottom-right corner.

(9) Sew the unit from step 8 to the bottom of the unit from step 7. Press the seam allowances open. Add a beige-solid 1½" x 8½" piece to the bottom of this unit. Press the seam allowances open.

10. Sew a beige-solid 2½" x 8½" piece to the left edge of the hat unit and a beige-solid 6" x 8½" piece to the right edge of the hat unit. Press the seam allowances toward the beige pieces.

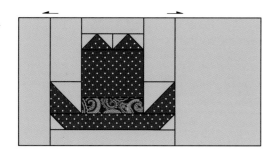

Make the Cowboy-Boots Unit

1. Draw a diagonal line from corner to corner on the wrong side of a beige-solid 2⅞" square. Layer the marked square on top of the medium-brown 2⅞" square, aligning the edges. Sew ¼" from both sides of the drawn line. Cut directly on the marked line to make two half-square-triangle units. Press the seam allowances toward the medium-brown fabric.

Make 2.

2. Sew a half-square-triangle unit from step 1 to one end of each of the remaining beige-solid 2½" x 4½" pieces as shown. Press the seam allowances toward the beige pieces.

3. Draw a diagonal line from corner to corner on the wrong side of four beige-solid 1½" squares. Place a marked square on the upper-left corner of a medium-brown 3½" x 5½" piece with the marked line oriented as shown. Sew on the marked line. Press the square up toward the

left corner. Place another marked square on the upper-right corner of the piece, orienting the marked line as shown. Sew on the marked line. Press the square up toward the right corner. Repeat to make a total of two units.

Make 2.

4. Add a beige-solid 1½" x 3½" piece to the top of each unit from step 4. Press the seam allowances toward the beige pieces.

5. Sew each unit from step 4 to a unit from step 2 as shown. Press the seam allowances open.

6. Refer to step 3 to mark four additional beige-solid 1½" squares and sew them to the ends of the medium-brown 1½" x 4½" pieces.

Make 2.

(7) Draw a diagonal line from corner to corner on the wrong side of the two beige-solid ½" squares. Place a marked square on the lower-right corner of a black 1½" square with the marked line oriented as shown. Sew on the marked line. Press the square down toward the corner. Repeat with the remaining marked square and black 1½" square, placing the marked square on the lower-left corner and orienting the marked line as shown.

(8) Join the units from step 7 to the ends of the units from step 6 as shown. Press the seam allowance open.

(9) Sew the units from step 8 to the bottom of the units from step 5 as shown. Press the seam allowances open. Add a beige-solid 1½" x 5½" piece to the bottom of each of these units. Press the seam allowances toward the beige pieces.

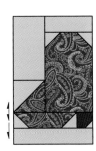 

(10) Sew a beige-solid 1½" x 8½" piece between the two boot units as shown. Press the seam allowances toward the beige piece.

Make the Bandanna Unit

(1) Draw a diagonal line from corner to corner on the wrong side of the beige-solid 4⅞" square. Layer the marked square on top of the blue 4⅞" square, aligning the edges. Sew ¼" from both sides of the drawn line. Cut directly on the marked line to make two half-square-triangle units. Press the seam allowances toward the blue fabric.

Make 2.

(2) Join the two half-square-triangle units as shown. Press the seam allowances open. Add the remaining beige-solid 1½" x 8½" piece to the bottom of this unit. Press the seam allowances toward the beige piece.

③ Draw a diagonal line from corner to corner on the wrong side of the remaining two beige-solid 1½" squares. Place a marked square on the left end of the blue 1½" x 8½" piece with the marked line oriented as shown. Sew on the marked line. Press the square up toward the left corner. Place another marked square on the right end of the piece, orienting the marked line as shown. Sew on the marked line. Press the square up toward the right corner.

④ Sew the unit from step 3 to the top of the unit from step 2. Press the seam allowances toward the unit from step 3. Add a beige-solid 2½" x 8½" piece to the top of the unit. Press the seam allowances toward the beige piece.

⑤ Sew the remaining beige-solid 6" x 8½" piece to the left side of the unit from step 4. Press the seam allowances toward the beige piece. Add the remaining beige-solid 2½" x 8½" piece to the right side of the unit. Press the seam allowances toward the beige piece.

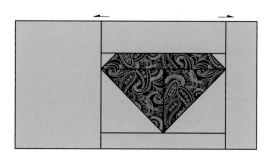

⑥ Trace the bandanna tie pattern (page 48) onto template plastic and cut it out. Fold the blue 4" x 12" piece in half, right sides together, to make a piece 4" x 6". Using the water-soluble pen and the tie template, trace two ties onto the folded fabric piece, aligning the short straight end with the fold. Cut out the pieces. Sew the tie pieces together, leaving a 3" opening for turning. Turn the piece right side out and tuck the seam allowances of the opening to the inside. Topstitch around the entire piece.

⑦ Press the tie in half crosswise. Place the tie crease directly on top of the diagonal seam at the upper-left corner of the bandanna unit. Sew on the crease, backstitching at the beginning and end of the stitching line.

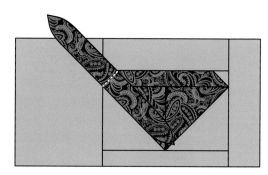

Align crease with seam; stitch.

Assemble the Hat, Boots, and Bandanna Row

Sew the completed hat, boots, and bandanna units together, referring to the photo (page 40) as needed. Press the seam allowances open.

Assemble the Quilt Top

① Sew the red 3½" x 42" strips together end to end to make one long strip. Press the seam allowances open. From the pieced strip, cut two strips, 3½" x 42½".

② Sew the red 7" x 42" strips together end to end to make one long strip. Press the seam allowances open. From the pieced strip, cut one strip, 7" x 42½".

③ Repeat step 2 with the beige print 7" x 42" strips.

④ Refer to the quilt assembly diagram below to sew the pieced rows and the red and beige print strips from steps 1–3 together. Press the seam allowances open.

⑤ Cut the jumbo rickrack into two pieces, 43" long. Using a wide zigzag stitch, sew the rickrack directly over the seams above and below the hat, boots, and bandanna row.

⑥ Cut the medium rickrack into six pieces, 43" long. Using a narrow zigzag stitch, sew the rickrack directly over each of the remaining seams between each row.

⑦ Tie the bandanna ties into a knot.

Appliqué the Stars

① Refer to "Fusible-Web Appliqué" (page 7) and use the star pattern (page 48) to prepare the appliqués from the remainder of the blue print.

② Fold the quilt top in half lengthwise and press a crease in the beige print strip to mark the center to use as a placement guide for the stars.

③ Center and appliqué the first star over the crease. Position and appliqué the remaining stars 7½" apart.

Finish the Quilt

① Refer to "Finishing Your Quilts" (page 8) to layer the quilt top with batting and backing; baste the layers together.

② Bind the quilt with the medium-brown 2½"-wide strips.

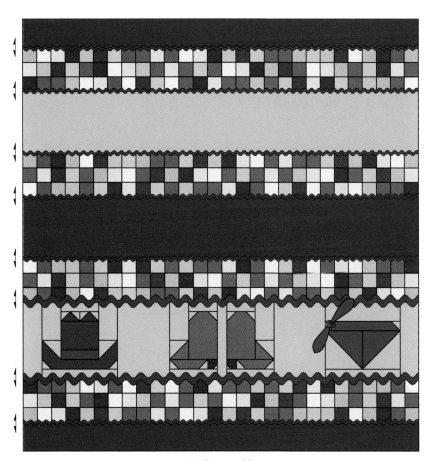

Quilt assembly

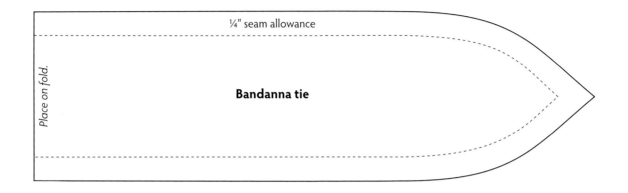

¼" seam allowance

Place on fold.

Bandanna tie

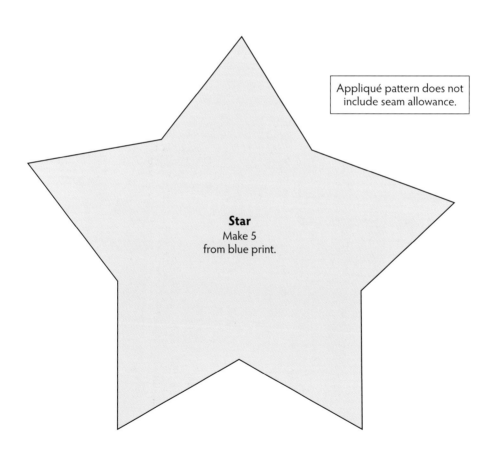

Appliqué pattern does not include seam allowance.

Star
Make 5
from blue print.

Rickrack Ruffles

Finished quilt: 42" x 42" • **Finished block:** 7½" x 7½"

Pieced by Kristin Roylance; machine quilted by Molly Kohler

This bright and frilly quilt is filled with rickrack and ruffles. It's all girl from top to bottom!

Materials

Yardage is based on 42"-wide fabric.
1⅓ yards of pink polka dot for ruffles and border
⅞ yard of pink-and-green stripe for blocks
⅝ yard of red tone on tone for flat piping and binding
⅔ yard of pink floral for blocks
2¾ yards of fabric for backing
50" x 50" piece of batting
6½ yards of green medium rickrack

Cutting

From the pink floral, cut:
10 strips, 2" x 42"

From the pink-and-green stripe, cut:
5 strips, 5" x 42"

From the pink polka dot, cut:
10 strips, 3" x 42"
2 strips, 2½" x 38"
2 strips, 2½" x 42"

From the red tone on tone, cut:
4 strips, ¾" x 42"
5 strips, 2½" x 42"

Make the Blocks

Use ¼"-wide seam allowances and sew with right sides together.

1. Sew a pink-floral strip to both long edges of a striped strip to make a strip set. Repeat to make a total of five strip sets. Press the seam allowances toward the pink-floral strips.

Make 5.

2. Press each of the strip sets from step 1 in half lengthwise to mark the lengthwise center.

3. Sew two polka-dot 3" x 42" strips together end to end to make one long strip. To keep the ends from fraying, either leave the selvages attached or trim them and apply a seam sealant to the edges. Repeat to make a total of five pieced strips.

4 Hem the long edges of each pieced strip from step 3 by pressing under the raw edges ¼" twice, and then sewing in place with a wide zigzag stitch.

5 Press each pieced strip from step 4 in half lengthwise to mark the lengthwise center. Hand or machine baste along the center crease of each strip, leaving long thread tails at the beginning and end. Pull the thread tails to gather each strip to 45". Secure the threads and evenly distribute the gathers.

6 Center a ruffled strip on the center crease of each strip set from step 1, right sides up. Sew through the center of the strips, stitching over the basting stitches.

7 Cut the rickrack into five 45" lengths. Center one length on each ruffle. Using a zigzag stitch, sew the rickrack to the ruffles.

8 Crosscut the strip sets into 25 segments, 8" wide, to complete the blocks.

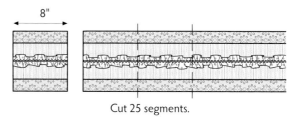

Cut 25 segments.

Assemble the Quilt Top

1 Refer to the quilt assembly diagram (page 52) to arrange the blocks into five rows of five blocks each, rotating the blocks in each row and from row to row to create the pattern. Sew the blocks in each row together, making sure you catch the ruffle ends of the horizontal blocks in the seam allowances. Press the seam allowances away from the ruffles. Trim any ruffle ends extending beyond the seam allowances. Sew the rows together, making sure you catch the ruffle ends of the vertical blocks in the seam allowances. Press the seam allowances open.

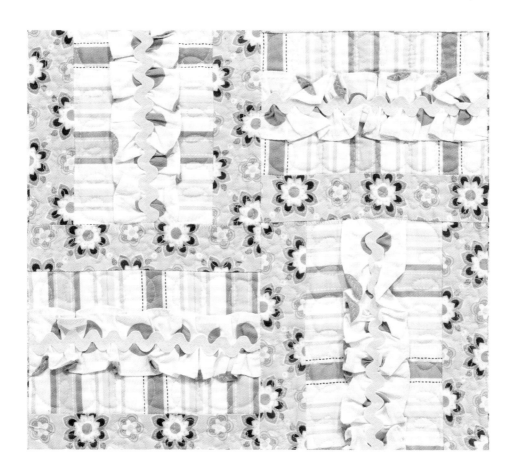

2. Press the red ¾" x 42" strips in half lengthwise, wrong sides together. With the fold toward the quilt center, baste two of the folded strips to the sides of the quilt top, ⅛" from the raw edges, having the excess strip extending at both ends. Trim the ends even with the quilt top and bottom edges. Baste the remaining two strips to the top and bottom of the quilt top in the same manner. Trim the ends even with the sides of the quilt top.

Trim.

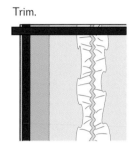

3. Sew the polka-dot 2½" x 38" border strips to the sides of the quilt top. Press the seam allowances toward the border strips. Sew the polka-dot 2½" x 42" strips to the top and bottom of the quilt top. Press the seam allowances toward the border strips.

Finish the Quilt

1. Refer to "Finishing Your Quilts" (page 8) to layer the quilt top with batting and backing; baste the layers together.

2. Bind the quilt with the red 2½"-wide strips.

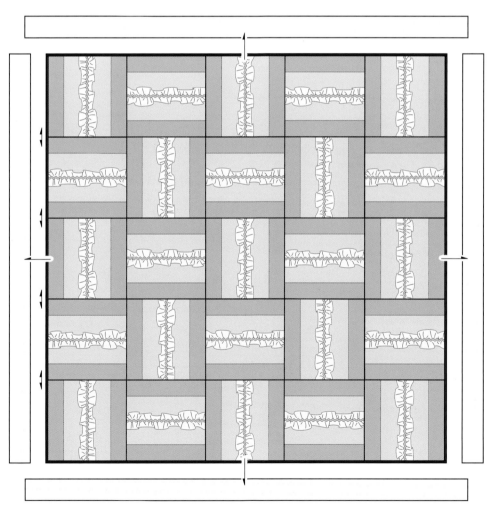

Quilt assembly

Tromp, Chomp, Stomp!

Finished quilt: 39½" x 42½"

Pieced by Kristin Roylance; machine quilted by Molly Kohler

Most children love dinosaurs, and these friendly dinos are sweet as can be! This fun quilt comes complete with prairie points for the dinosaur spikes. These dinosaurs will tromp, chomp, and stomp their way into your little one's heart!

Materials

Yardage is based on 42"-wide fabric.

¼ yard *each* of 8 assorted blue, green, orange, yellow, and gray prints for pieced quilt center and prairie points

1⅛ yards of dark-brown solid for appliqué background and inner and outer borders

¼ yard of orange tone on tone for pieced quilt center and tall-dinosaur appliqué

¼ yard of blue tone on tone for pieced quilt center and short-dinosaur appliqué

¼ yard of small-scale blue print for pieced quilt center and tall-dinosaur-spikes appliqué

¼ yard of green polka dot for pieced quilt center and tree-top, bushes, and short-dinosaur-spikes appliqués

⅛ yard of medium-brown print for tree-trunk appliqué

⅛ yard of gray print for rock and tall-dinosaur-tummy appliqués

½ yard of coordinating stripe for binding

2⅝ yards of fabric for backing

47" x 50" piece of batting

½ yard of 17"-wide paper-backed fusible web

4 black ¼"-diameter buttons for dinosaur eyes

Cutting

From *each* of the 8 assorted blue, green, orange, yellow, and gray prints, cut:
1 strip, 3½" x 42"; crosscut into 11 squares, 3½" x 3½" (88 total)

From the orange tone on tone, cut:
1 strip, 3½" x 42"; crosscut into 11 squares, 3½" x 3½"

From the blue tone on tone, cut:
1 strip, 3½" x 42"; crosscut into 11 squares, 3½" x 3½"

From the small-scale blue print, cut:
1 strip, 3½" x 42"; crosscut into 11 squares, 3½" x 3½"
1 strip, 2½" x 42"; crosscut into 5 squares, 2½" x 2½"

From the green polka dot, cut:
1 strip, 3½" x 42"; crosscut into 11 squares, 3½" x 3½"
1 strip, 2½" x 42"; crosscut into 6 squares, 2½" x 2½"

From the dark-brown solid, cut:
1 strip, 6½" x 27½"
8 strips, 3½" x 42"; crosscut into:
  • 2 strips, 3½" x 27½"
  • 4 strips, 3½" x 36½"
  • 2 strips, 3½" x 39"

From the stripe, cut:
5 strips, 2½" x 42"

Piece the Quilt Center

Use ¼"-wide seam allowances and sew with right sides together.

① Using the assorted print, orange tone-on-tone, blue tone-on-tone, small-scale blue, and small-scale green 3½" squares, randomly sew nine squares together side by side to make a row. Press the seam allowances open. Repeat to make a total of eight rows.

Make 8 rows.

2. Sew six rows together along the long edges to make the top section. Press the seam allowances open. Sew the remaining two rows together along the long edges to make the bottom section. Press the seam allowances open.

3. Sew the top section to the top of the dark-brown 6½" x 27½" strip. Sew the bottom section to the bottom of the dark-brown strip. Press the seam allowances toward the brown strip.

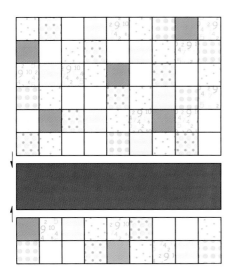

Add the Borders

1. Add the dark-brown 3½" x 27½" inner-border strips to the top and bottom of the pieced center. Press the seam allowances toward the brown strips. Sew dark-brown 3½" x 36½" inner-border strips to the sides of the center. Press the seam allowances toward the brown strips.

2. Select 46 of the remaining 3½" squares and press each one in half diagonally, wrong sides together. Press each one in half again to make the large prairie points for the border. Set aside the remaining 3½" squares for another project.

Fold.   Fold.   Make 46.

3. Repeat step 2 with the small-scale green and small-scale blue 2½" squares to make 11 small prairie points for the dinosaur spikes.

4. Randomly select 12 large prairie points and lay them out on an inner side border, aligning the raw edges. The point of each prairie point should align with the center of a square. Tuck the corner of each prairie point into the opening of the prairie point next to it. Pin; then baste the prairie points in place. Repeat for the opposite side border.

5. Randomly select 11 large prairie points and repeat step 4 to baste them to the top border, making sure the edges of the corner prairie points align as shown. Repeat for the bottom border.

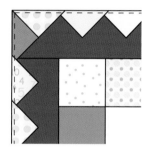

Baste prairie points in place along raw edges.

6. Sew the remaining dark-brown 3½" x 36½" border strips to the sides of the quilt top. Press the seam allowances toward the quilt center. Sew the dark-brown 3½" x 39" border strips to the top and bottom of the quilt top. Press the seam allowances toward the quilt center.

Appliqué the Quilt Top

1. Refer to "Fusible-Web Appliqué" (page 7) and use the patterns (pages 57–59) to prepare the appliqués from the fabrics indicated.

2. Referring to the photo (page 53) for placement, appliqué the pieces to the quilt top in the following order: tree trunk, tree top, rock, medium bush, and small bush.

3. Determine the placement of each of the dinosaurs and pin them in place. *Do not appliqué them yet.*

4. With the opening of the prairie point facing toward the right, line up the six small green prairie points across the back of the short dinosaur, tucking the corners of the prairie points into the opening of the prairie point to the left and tucking the raw edges under the dinosaur ¼". Pin the prairie points in place. Remove the dinosaur and baste the prairie points to the quilt top. Repeat with the five small blue prairie points and the tall dinosaur.

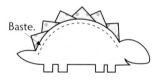

Baste.

Baste.

5. Appliqué the remaining prepared pieces to the quilt top in the following order: short dinosaur, tall dinosaur tummy, tall dinosaur, large bush.

6. Securely attach the four black buttons to the dinosaurs where indicated for the eyes. If this quilt is for a very small child, consider drawing in the eyes with a permanent marker to eliminate a choking hazard.

Finish the Quilt

1. Refer to "Finishing Your Quilts" (page 8) to layer the quilt top with batting and backing; baste the layers together.

2. Bind the quilt with the striped 2½"-wide strips.

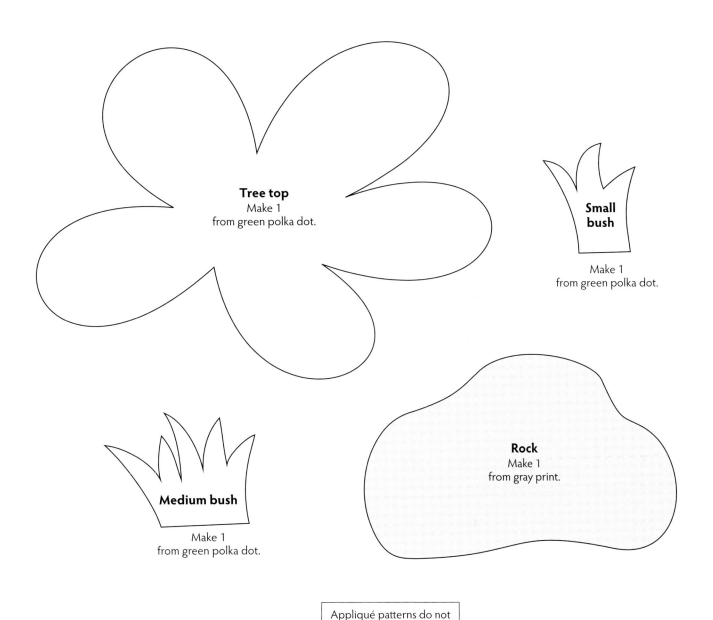

Tree top
Make 1
from green polka dot.

Small bush
Make 1
from green polka dot.

Medium bush
Make 1
from green polka dot.

Rock
Make 1
from gray print.

Appliqué patterns do not include seam allowances.

Button
placement.

Short dinosaur
Make 1
from blue tone on tone.

Appliqué patterns do not
include seam allowances.

Tree trunk
Make 1
from medium-brown print.

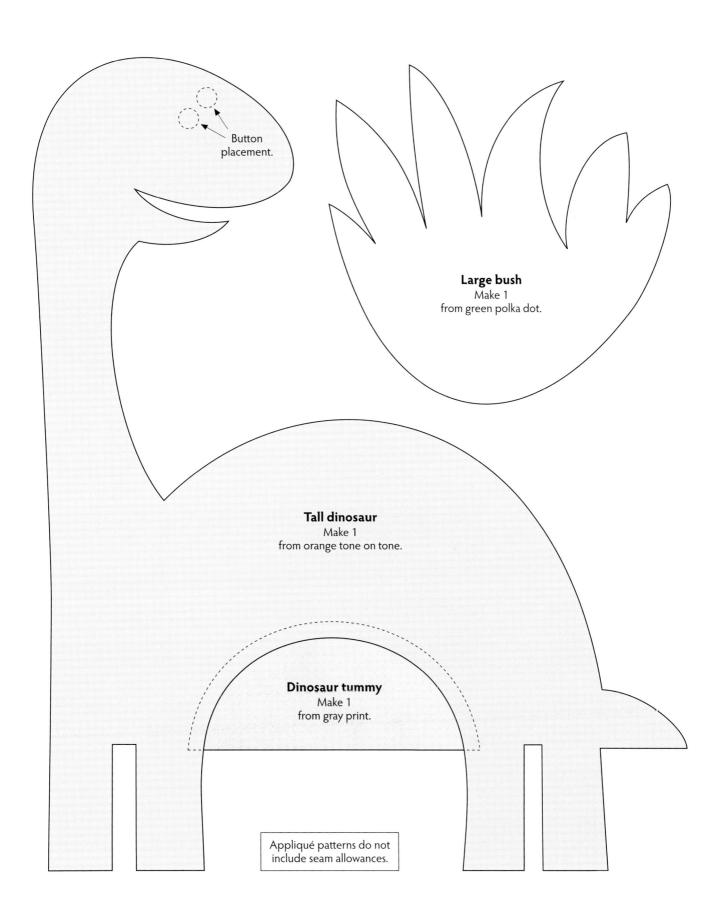

Button placement.

Large bush
Make 1
from green polka dot.

Tall dinosaur
Make 1
from orange tone on tone.

Dinosaur tummy
Make 1
from gray print.

Appliqué patterns do not
include seam allowances.

Tutu Cute

Finished quilt: 41½" x 48½"

Pieced by Kristin Roylance; machine quilted by Molly Kohler

Big, bold prints and sweet tulle tutus make this quilt just too, too cute!

Materials

Yardage is based on 42"-wide fabric unless otherwise specified.

⅓ yard *each* of 4 assorted large-scale prints for focus strips

¾ yard of dark-brown batik for contrast strips and binding

⅔ yard of 54"-wide dark-brown tulle

½ yard of white solid for background

2¾ yards of fabric for backing

50" x 57" piece of batting

5" x 5" square of paper-backed fusible web

2½ yards of dark-brown jumbo rickrack

Water-soluble pen

Cutting

From the dark-brown batik, cut:

3 strips, 3½" x 42"

5 strips, 2½" x 42"

From *each* of the 4 assorted large-scale prints, cut:

1 strip, 8½" x 42"

From the white solid, cut:

1 strip, 11½" x 41½"

From the tulle, cut:

4 strips, 5" x 54"

Assemble the Quilt Top

Use ¼"-wide seam allowances and sew with right sides together.

1. Alternately sew the large-scale print strips and dark-brown 3½" strips together along the long edges to make a strip set. Press the seam allowances toward the dark-brown strips. Crosscut the strip set into one piece, 28½" wide, and one piece, 9½" wide. Set aside the remainder of the strip set for the appliquéd circles.

Make 1 strip set.
Cut 1 piece, 28½" wide, and 1 piece, 9½" wide.

2. Using the water-soluble pen, mark vertical lines on the right side of the white strip: 4¼", 15¼", 26¼", and 37¼" from the left edge.

③ Sew the short ends of a tulle strip together to create a circle. Fold the piece in half lengthwise, with the seam allowances on the inside. Hand baste ¼" from the fold, leaving long thread tails at the beginning and end.

④ Pull the tails to gather the tulle strip tightly and evenly so that the center opening measures 1" in diameter. Knot the thread ends to secure the gathers.

⑤ Repeat steps 3 and 4 to make a total of four gathered tulle "tutu" rings.

⑥ Sew each of the finished tulle rings to the center of the marked lines on the white strip. Follow the manufacturer's instructions to remove the drawn lines.

⑦ Refer to "Fusible-Web Appliqué" (page 7) and use the circle pattern to prepare the appliqués. Appliqué a fabric circle to the center of each tulle ring in the same order as the 28½"-wide strip unit, referring to the photo as needed.

⑧ Refer to the quilt assembly diagram on page 63 to sew the 28½" pieced unit from step 1 to the top of the white strip. Press the seam allowances toward the pieced unit. Sew the 9½" piece to the bottom of the white strip. Press the seam allowances toward the pieced unit.

9. Cut the rickrack into two 45" lengths. Center a length over the seams between the pieced sections and the white strip. Stitch through the center of each length using a wide zigzag stitch. Trim the rickrack ends even with the quilt sides.

Finish the Quilt

1. Refer to "Finishing Your Quilts" (page 8) to layer the quilt top with batting and backing; baste the layers together.

2. Bind the quilt with the brown 2½"-wide strips.

Quilt assembly

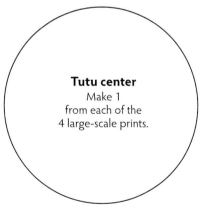

Tutu center
Make 1
from each of the
4 large-scale prints.

Appliqué pattern does not
include seam allowance.

Acknowledgments

My sincere thanks and genuine appreciation to:

My talented machine quilter, Molly Kohler, who is somehow able to "see" a quilt before she ever starts stitching. Her work is meticulous and magically transforms a simple quilt top into an amazing work of art to be treasured for generations!

The Martingale team, for taking a chance on me.

Riley Blake Designs, for allowing me to use their beautiful fabric in many of my quilts. They are a pleasure to work with, and generous with their time, insight, and fabric.

The numerous quilters that have shared their talents with me, especially my grandmother, Rhea Blessing. She allowed me to quilt with her when I was a young girl, and instilled in me a love for the genuine beauty of a handmade gift from the heart.

About the Author

My very first introduction to quilting came while visiting my grandmother's home as a young child. I can remember sitting under a quilting frame, carefully pushing a needle back up for my sister to pull through from the top. We were quite the team! I remember going home with bandages on each and every fingertip, but I couldn't wait to try it again. My next notable quilting experience also included bandages . . . this time with a trip to the emergency room. Rotary blades can be very dangerous! I've learned a lot and rarely require Band-Aids these days.

I started my pattern company, Cute Quilt Patterns, in 2008. I've enjoyed the many friendships that come from daily interactions with fellow quilters. I love having the opportunity to share my designs and being able to see the creativity they inspire.

I am blessed to live on a beautiful hillside of the Wasatch mountains in Utah with my amazing husband and six energetic, quilt-toting children. Visit me online at www.CuteQuiltPatterns.com.

64